# Love and Charity

## THE LIFE AND STORY OF LOUISE HUNTER
### AND THE LOVE AND CHARITY HOMELSS SHELTER

BY

DENNIS JAMES WOODS

LIFE TO LEGACY

Love and Charity:
The Life and Story of Louise Hunter and
the Love and Charity Homeless Shelter

Copyright © 2005 by: Dennis James Woods

ISBN-13: 978-1-947288-42-3

Second Edition (2018)

All rights reserved solely by the author. Except where designated, the author certifies that all contents are original and do not infringe upon the legal rights of any other person. No part of this book may be reproduced in any form without permission in writing from the publisher, except in the case of brief quotations embodied in critical articles or reviews.

All scriptural references are from or based on the authorized King James Version.

Printed in the United States of America

10 9 8 7 6 5 4 3 2 1

Cover design by: Legacy Designs, Inc.
                Legacydesigninc@gmail.com

The photographs in this book are used with the permission of the Journal Times, Racine Wisconsin, Editor Randy Brant, Mark Hertzberg director of photography:

Published by:
Life To Legacy, LLC
P.O. Box 1239
Matteson, IL 60443
877-267-7477
www.Life2Legacy.com

# TABLE OF CONTENTS

Chapters

| | |
|---|---|
| Preface | 4 |
| Introduction | 11 |
| 1. Humble Beginnings | 15 |
| 2. The Years In Vicksburg | 28 |
| 3. The Trials of Marriage | 43 |
| 4. The Land of Promise and Pain | 55 |
| 5. Manifest Destiny | 78 |
| 6. A Shelter is Born | 91 |
| 7. Mission Impossible | 110 |
| 8. Remembrances | 141 |
| 9. The House of Hope | 165 |
| 10. Image of a Godly Woman | 181 |
| Epilogue | 194 |

# Preface

In early 1992, I was affiliated with the Chicago Victory Center, an outreach ministry on Chicago's northwest side. This ministry was known for both its discipleship programs and its fine men's homes. After a brief counseling session with Pastor Fernando Rivas, pastor of the Victory Center, it was suggested that I attend a week of revival in St. Louis. There in St. Louis, Pastor Rivas' brother Joey Rivas pastored a very similar ministry. Pastor Rivas assured me that after I returned from St. Louis, I would be assigned to one of the men's homes that the Victory Center operated. This was all welcomed news, and a few days later, I was on my way to St. Louis Missouri.

After returning from St. Louis, I heard that the Victory Center operated a men's home in Wisconsin, in a small town named Racine. Sensing the prompting of the Holy Spirit, I asked the senior pastor if I could go to the men's home in Wisconsin. To my surprise, he readily agreed to let me go. I was so excited about the fact that I was going to a place where I hadn't been to before. I've always loved going to new places. Therefore, with great anticipation, I couldn't wait to see what my new home was going to be like. So later that same evening, I boarded the church van and was on my way to Racine.

When we arrived, I immediately fell in love with it. It wasn't congested nor was there all the hustle and bustle typically found in Chicago. It was a much smaller town with only eighty thousand people. Unlike some of the Victory Center's men's homes, which were based out of apartment buildings and storefronts, here in Racine, the ministry was based out of a former nightclub which had been converted into a church. The building was fairly large and could accommodate at least two hundred people. It had a beautiful sanctuary and also had a large kitchen and dining room.

Shortly after getting settled in, it was close to suppertime, and I had mustered up a hefty appetite. One of the things I noticed right away was that dinner consisted of a wide range of food items. It was almost like a feast. There were meats, fresh produce, all sorts of pastries and other bakery items. Yes, that first supper was a wonderful meal, and we all enjoyed ourselves eating until we were full.

After finishing supper, I remember asking the director of the men's home, "Where did we get so much food?"

He told me, "We get our food and clothes from a lady named Mother Hunter. Mother Hunter operates the Love and Charity mission here in town and she's the one who gives us plenty of everything we need. We all thank God for Mother Hunter. If it were not for her, I don't know where we'd get our food and clothes."

I remember being immediately impressed with her. She sounded like a very gracious woman. After hearing so many good things, I had a desire to meet her.

After a few weeks had passed, it was time to pick up supplies from the mission again, so I anxiously volunteered for the detail. We loaded up several boxes into our van and I road over to the mission with one of the men's home counselors. When we arrived at the mission, I saw many tables lined along the front of the mission, filled with various food and clothing items. I remember asking Kevin, "Does she leave this food out here for just anybody to get?"

And he responded, "Yes. That's how she does it."

So we got out of our van, unloaded our boxes and walked into the mission. As soon as we walked through the door, I heard this woman's voice call out, "Hey there, how yawl doing?"

And that's when I saw her for the very first time. It was Mrs. Louise Hunter. The counselor returned the greeting and then went on to introduce me. "Mrs. Hunter, I'd like you to meet someone. His name is Brother Dennis Woods. He's also from Chicago. He just joined our ministry a few weeks ago, and I thought it would be nice for him to meet you."

Mother Hunter then asked me, How I was doing? I told her that I was doing fine and was glad to be here in Racine. Then she asked us to have a seat and offered us a cup of coffee and some sweet rolls. So we gladly obliged her hospitality and took our seats as she prepared us a delicious continental breakfast. After our coffee and pastries were served, Mother Hunter asked me to tell her about myself. I intended to say only a few things, but I ended up telling her what seemed like my whole life's story. She was so easy to open up to.

There was something about Mother Hunter that was so lovingly inviting. Her love and tenderness were hard to resist and could just draw out even the most reserved, introverted individual.

After hearing my testimony, she began to counsel and encourage me. She told me that God had an important work for me to do, but I must wait on the Lord, and in time, He would bring the desires of my heart to pass. Then she looked over to the counselor and asked him if he would ask the Pastor if I could come to preach at one of the Sunday evening services. The counselor told her he would do just that. Shortly after that, we finished loading up the van and returned to the men's home.

I'll never forget that first day that I met Louise Hunter. There was such an atmosphere of love and blessing all around her. I just knew that I'd been in the presence of someone who was really special. And

# Love and Charity

I thanked God for opening this wonderful door of blessing for me there at Love and Charity. I was elated that Mother Hunter wanted me to preach for her at the mission. I could hardly wait for the opportunity to preach my first sermon in Racine.

Approximately one month later, I did get the opportunity to preach at Love and Charity, and ever since that Sunday night service, Mother Hunter and I had a special bond.

Some months later, in November 1992, I returned to preach once again at the mission. After the service was over, Mother Hunter and I were having supper and she asked me to come to help her run the mission. She said she needed a man who could live at the mission and watch over things. She also told me how it would be a great blessing for me if I came to help her. Mother Hunter went on to say my being there would take a load off her back. She then promised me "if you will serve the Lord here for a while, you will never regret it."

Not wanting to make up my mind hastily, I sought the Lord in prayer. A few days later, I felt that the Lord was leading me to serve Him here at Love and Charity. So on December 31, 1992, I left the Victory Center and took up an assistant's position at the mission. This is where my close association with this anointed woman of God, all began.

In the months that I spent serving the Lord at Love and Charity, I became a better minister. The knowledge I gained there I could not have learned at a seminary, or from textbooks, or even in a local church. I learned what commitment to ministry and hard work was all about. In addition to all that, I learned what sacrifice was all about, and the leadership it takes to run a homeless shelter. I was truly blessed that God led me to Love and Charity. Mother Hunter and I had a wonderful relationship as I worked side by side with her on a daily basis. The wonderful things I experienced at Love and Charity have had a profound impact on my life. And to this day I'm a better man and minister because of time I spent meeting the needs of God's people there at Love and Charity.

When I first stepped foot in Love and Charity, I didn't realize that I would be writing Mother Hunter's biography, but then, someone had to do it. Her story is a great American story. In a world of so many negative stereotypes, people need to know about one of America's greatest African-American women.

Though many have set out to tell the story of Louise Hunter and the Love and Charity Homeless Shelter, the Lord appointed me to this high honor. Therefore, I am grateful to The Lord, Mrs. Hunter, and the Love and Charity Mission for being a part of my life. I am therefore very proud to present, *Love and Charity, The Life and Story of Louise Hunter, and the Love and Charity Homeless Shelter.*

Though this is a factual biographical work and because it's so amazingly entertaining, I consider it a biographical drama. And though this book is based on a true story, it was necessary to be considerate of some of the characters' privacy and anonymity, therefore many of their names have been changed. Also, in order to maintain continuity throughout this account, particularly where obtaining direct quotes were not possible, many of the conversations, situations, and commentary were added by the author. However, all the stories were actually told to me by Mrs. Hunter according to her best recollection of how the events portrayed in this book occurred.

It is by design that I have chosen to write this biographical account in the first person. Though I realize that biographies are normally written in third person, I wanted the reader to be impacted by the accounts just as I was on the various occasions when she would share them with me. When Mother Hunter would tell her story, it was in first person. When she described the scenes of the fiery plane crash, it was in the first person. When she recounted the tragic fire that claimed the life of her son, it was in the first person. All of the poignant accounts of this story were portrayed in the first person. Since I experienced a range of emotions from this story, I wanted the reader to experience her joy and pain, just as I did when she recounted the events of her life.

Therefore, I didn't want to give *Love and Charity* to the readers in a third person account, as biographies are typically portrayed. To me, it was equally important that the reader experience her up close then to simply see through the eyes of another. I wanted you to be there walking in her shoes, not just reading about where it was that she walked. The style that I have chosen to write this book is for the purpose of effect. I did not approach this book on the basis of a court reporter's word-for-word account. I took the license to write this account through the lens of my own emotions. In a sense I became her as I wrote. I did this because I was personally involved with Mother Hunter on a day-to-day basis. I lived and worked alongside her at the Love and Charity Homeless Shelter. I was not a casual observer. I was an insider. I was there.

It took ten long years to finish this book. Though it was actually completed in 1994, this work was not ready at that time. I had to mature to a level that was worthy of this story. Yes, it was necessary for me to mature as a person and a writer before Love and Charity could be given to you, the reader. It is therefore, my prayer and sincere hope that this book has an impact on your life as it has on mine.

***Love:** A deep and tender feeling of affection for or attachment or devotion to a person or persons, a feeling of brotherhood and good will towards other people.*

***Charity:** An act of goodwill or affection of man for his fellow man, kindness or leniency in judging others, a voluntary giving of money or other help to those in need.*

–New World Dictionary, Second College Edition

# Introduction

In the beautiful city of Racine, just blocks away from downtown's Monument Square, there is an inconspicuous two-story brown brick building on the corner of Douglas and Prospect Avenue.

To the casual observer, there is nothing obvious about this location that would lead one to think miracles take place inside. Yet the word around town is, miracles have been performed there. Yes, countless lives have been changed for the better. Unlike your typical restaurant or department store, you won't find any neon signs or elaborate marquees to lure in the curious. You'll simply see a humble little sign that says, Love and Charity.

If you observe this place for any length of time, you'd notice a high amount of foot traffic entering and exiting practically all hours of the day. You'll also see vehicles pull up, one after the other, with their occupants scurrying inside. Soon you'd see them leave with hefty boxes of food, enough food to feed an entire family for a whole week. Still, others come and may leave with clothes, appliances or furniture. Amongst the comings and goings of these everyday people, a street and sanitation truck stops right in front and begins honking his horn. Suddenly, someone darts out of the building carrying a simmering breakfast sandwich, and a hot cup of coffee. He hands it to the driver who then says, "Thanks again!" waves goodbye and pulls away. Now, if curiosity starts to get the best of you, you'll want to take a tour of this interesting place. Let's go inside.

As soon as you enter, you see a sizable kitchen, and you smell the aroma of delectable meals being prepared. You also see dedicated volunteer workers packing boxes full of meats, bakery items, and produce. All these wholesome commodities will soon be distributed to those in need throughout the community.

On the other side of the kitchen, you see a newly constructed dining facility. The first thing that would grab your attention is how well it's decorated. Like that of an elegant restaurant, those who eat there would feel privileged. Inside the dining room, there are beautiful plants in floor pottery as well as flowers hanging down from the ceiling. There are many beautiful paintings hanging on the walls and there is soft Gospel music playing over the stereo system. The tables are dressed with beautiful tablecloths, and each place is neatly set up. If you continue through this facility, you'll see the glorious chapel area. There are a beautifully dressed altar and pulpit decked with radiant red carpet. There's a piano, organ and a drum set, to enhance the worship services. And, there are enough church pews to accommodate at least two hundred worshipers.

As we continue on our tour, you'll come to a set of stairs that lead up to the second floor. Once upstairs you would see, several sleeping rooms all neat and clean. Each has a large twin-sized bed dressed in beautiful bed linen. The beds are all neatly made, and you'll also notice an open Bible resting up against the pillows. The floors are clean and swept and all the rooms have fresh spring-like fragrance. Everything is in an orderly arrangement and is well maintained.

As I have described thus far, one gets the impression of a multifaceted facility. At first, you may have thought that I was describing a neighborhood food store. Although people come here to get groceries, it's not a local grocer. But then again, you may have thought I was describing a department store. Though many people have come here to get clothes, furniture, and appliances, it's not a part of any national retail chain. There's even a chance that you may have thought I was describing some local church. Although there's a pulpit, a chapel, and daily worship services, this is not a local church either.

But wait, there's something or shall I say, *someone* else that also fits into this picture. Each morning at approximately ten o'clock, you'll see a gray sedan, pull up and park right in front of the entrance. Out of it steps a modestly dressed woman of African-American descent. She closes her car door and makes her way to the entrance, but she hesitates before she goes in. Then with a discriminating eye, she gives the outside of the building a good looking over.

Now even to the most casual observer, you can't help notice there's a peculiar radiance about her. Though there's an air of humility about her, confidence emits from her small slender frame. Although she may not look it, she's the mother of nineteen living children and the grandmother of over eighty grandchildren. Who is she? Her name is Louise Hunter. What's this place I've been describing? It's the Love and Charity Homeless Shelter.

The scene that I've just described to you hasn't always been this way, you know. What's here today all came by faith and many years of hard work. For years Louise Hunter has fed the hungry and housed the homeless. What you're reading about now all started over thirty years ago, right from the confines of her home here in Racine, Wisconsin. Personally acquainted with sorrow and grief, I tell Louise's poignant story of how all of this came to be, stemming back to the cotton fields of Warren County Mississippi, in the early 1930s. Her captivating story reveals her victories and her failures, her triumphs and her defeats, all dramatically told by her family members, and associates alike.

Although some might say that there are no real heroes in the world today, I would certainly beg to differ with them. Though faced with many years of trials and tribulations, through it all, Louise Hunter has emerged as one of America's greatest crusaders for the cause of the homeless. Being a woman of great faith, she is also a legend in her own time. Truly, her humanitarian contributions to the homeless and socially disadvantaged can be summed up in just three words, *Love and Charity…*

## Chapter 1

## Humble Beginnings

Louise Hunter was born Louise Strong on June 14, 1934. She was the second eldest of four children born to Carrie and Andrew Strong. The Strong's were hard-working sharecroppers, who lived on a small farm, far out in the countryside, thirty or so miles from the historic city of Vicksburg, Mississippi. Louise had three siblings. There were her two sisters, Margret and Vergie, and her brother Andrew Junior.

Louise and her family dwelt in a humble little old farmhouse, which was in disrepair and barely habitable. However, as Louise described it, it was the house that the Lord had given. During the 1930s when Louise was raised, America was in the midst of the hard economic times of the Great Depression. People were starving and living in the streets. Therefore, the Strongs were thankful for the little they had. Though their little house was not much to be desired, many people had nowhere to sleep at all, so they appreciated having a warm place to lay their heads at night.

As Louise reached back into her memory, she described their house as a little white-frame house, the type of house typically found throughout the South in those days. Around their little farmhouse was a wire fence that encircled the yard where there was plenty of grass and shrubs, shade trees and wild flowers. They had no electricity, natural gas nor running water, therefore everything that was done in the house and around the farm was done manually without the aid of appliances or machinery.

These primitive surroundings set the stage for the making of one of America's greatest contemporary humanitarians. As Louise begins to recall it:

I can still remember waking up early in the morning to the sounds of roosters crowing in the yard and the clamor of pots and pans in the kitchen as Mama prepared breakfast for us. The aroma of country eggs and sausage filled the fresh morning air, as they sizzled on top of our wood-burning stove. With raging appetites, we hurried to get washed and dressed so we could eat the scrumptious breakfast. Mmm, it still makes my mouth water just to think of sopping Mama's homemade biscuits in her delicious brown gravy. I really miss eating the food that we raised on our farm. Unlike the food purchased in today's stores that's days old, we were fortunate enough to eat farm fresh food, which kept our young bodies, well-nourished and healthy.

Now while we were having breakfast, Daddy had been up long before us tending to the farm. I can't ever recall having seen Daddy in bed by the time we got up. On a rare occasion Daddy might sleep in a while when he was sick, but other than that, he was up working the farm. Yes, my daddy was a man's man. He was of a dark complexion, only average height, and medium build but, when Daddy spoke we all listened. Daddy certainly spoke his mind, and wouldn't take any back talk from us, at all. Although he could be rather firm at times, Daddy was a very compassionate man, who was God-fearing and only wanting the best for his family. He raised us up in the fear of the Lord, believing what the Scriptures teach, that if you train a child in the way they should go, when they are old they will not depart from it.[1]

Yes, Daddy worked very hard to provide for us. He would be up plowing, planting, and feeding the animals long before sunrise and often kept working till after sunset. On nights when there was a full moon, just to get caught up, Daddy would even work by the moonlight. But as hard as Daddy worked, he was fortunate to break even every year. He often had to borrow money on the hopes of the next year's crops, to make limited purchases at the general store in Vicksburg. Doing this always kept us behind. Unfortunately, we were already in debt before the next season had even begun. Sadly, when you consider, all the toil and the sweat of my father's brow, there was no profit in sharecropping another man's land. A mule and forty acres, it wasn't a lot to look forward to.

There's no doubt about it. Daddy had a lot of pressure on him, especially being black and living in Mississippi back during the 1930s. If it were not for his faith in God and the love he had for his family, I don't know if Daddy could have continued on the way he did. Thank God Daddy was not a quitter. Once he set his mind to do something, he was not one to give up easily. He was not like so many other men that abandoned their families and all their responsibilities. The Lord blessed us with a good father who stood firm through thick and thin, whether in good times or bad times, Daddy was always there.

Now as the saying goes, *Behind every good man there is a good woman to support him.* This was certainly the case when it came to my mother Mrs. Carrie Strong. Now Mama was a strong and supportive woman who was also very sweet and kind. She had long black hair, was of a medium build, and her complexion was brown and her skin was smooth. She was very sweet and tender-hearted and she had strong convictions and belief in the Lord.

After preparing breakfast for us and getting us off to school, she would leave home and work as a housekeeper. After a long day's work cleaning up white folks' homes, she would find the strength to tend to us back at the farm. She seemed to be so tireless, but in reality, she wasn't. The fact is Mama was driven by her dedication to her family, who she loved so much. However, little did I know at the time, that one day, I would experience what it's like to be driven by the power of love and to be dedicated to a cause.

Being raised during the Great Depression era, there was hardly any money available. We were so poor that my parents could not afford to buy us clothes. Therefore, Mama had to be very resourceful, and make our clothes from whatever material she could find. Most of our clothes were made from flour sacks she would save up throughout the year. Under these circumstances, we obviously didn't have fancy clothes, but the clothes we did have mama kept mended and clean.

Early Saturday mornings, part of our chores was to help Mama do laundry. Mama would use a big black iron kettle to wash the laundry in. After filling the kettle with water drawn from the nearby Bear Creek, it was necessary to boil our clothes to loosen the dirt. So Mama would set a fire underneath the kettle to bring the water to a boil. After boiling a bundle of clothes for a while, Mama carefully removed those steaming clothes from the kettle with a pitchfork and placed them in a tub so she could scrub them using her homemade lye soap.

Mama's lye soap could clean clothes just as well as detergents you find in the stores today. She made this amazing soap by cooking a mixture of animal fat and lye. After the soap had simmered a bit, she would let it cool off and then pour it into molds. Once it had hardened, it would turn white as snow and she'd cut it out in squares so she could store it away. Though Mama's homemade soap was perfect for cleaning our clothes, I found out the hard way that it was too harsh for us to bathe with. The lye in the soap was an irritant and would make your skin burn something awful.

After Mama washed our clothes, she would hang them out to dry in the fresh country air. Soon after drying, she would iron them, using one of those old heavy steel irons that had to be heated up in the fire.

As heavy as that old rusty iron was, mama, got it to work just fine. She took just as much care cleaning and ironing our clothes as she did for the white folks. Looking back at it, during the times we were raised everything seemed to be a task, but we accepted life on its own terms and didn't do much complaining.

During the school year, each day we had to walk miles to and from school. It was quite an adventure to say the least. Back in those days, out in the country, there were no sidewalks, paved roads or streets. In order to get to school, we walked down dirt roads and trails, over hills, through the hollows and woods. It was so scary at times. When the wind would whistle through the trees and thickets, or we would hear the sounds of critters as they scurried through the underbrush, our vivid imaginations would often run wild. However, not all of our fears were spurred from our imaginations. There were wild animals that lived in those wooded areas, and on occasion, we would encounter wild dogs or even a bear. But most of the time we played to and from school, being the typical carefree children, completely oblivious to the dangers that lurked in the backwoods of Warren County.

After our adventurous journey, we finally arrived at our little schoolhouse right before class started. Though I cannot recall the name of the school, I do remember that grades one through six all met in this small one-room schoolhouse. However, I still remember Ms. Lucille Olley, the meanest teacher I ever had. Most of the kids in school were afraid of her. If you acted out on Ms. Olley, she'd come across your backside with a switch. She certainly believed in classroom discipline, and young 'ins getting their lesson. It was Ms. Olley who taught me how to read and write. Yes, I enjoyed going to school because it was about the only other time I got to be around other children. However, during the springtime, when planting season came, we had to stay behind to help plant cotton. We could go weeks, even months on end without having gone to school one day.

During the summer, my sisters, brother and I would all find the time to play when we could. But as you may know, there's a lot of work to do around a farm, especially when it was time to harvest our cotton crops. Boy did I ever hate to pick that old cotton, and me being so lazy didn't help matters much either. After filling my sack with just enough cotton to make me a comfortable little cushion, I'd lay down on it and go to sleep. My older sister Margaret would get mad because, while I was off snoozing somewhere, she would have to do all the work herself.

At the age of nine, I was the typical mischievous little child. Being a little tattle teller and sticking my nose in everybody else's business, I once told Mama that my older sister Margaret was kissing one of the boys back during the school year. So Margaret got even with me by locking me in a chest and leaving me there practically all day. I was so scared in that old dark chest. I thought I was going to die. No matter how hard I kicked or how loud I screamed, Margret sat on that chest and wouldn't let me out. After a while, when I settled down, Margret went on her way as though nothing had happened. However, it didn't take too long before Mama missed me, and when no one else saw me around, Mama was worried sick.

She frantically searched everywhere for me. Then finally, she came upon the chest was out behind the house. Something must have told her to look inside and when she did, there I was curled up and sound asleep. Poor Mama screamed thinking that I was dead. When she screamed, it startled me and there I came jumping up out of that chest. That's when I told her what Margret did. Mama got so mad, she went and got the rifle and fired a few rounds in the air, as Margaret ran for her life out across the cotton field. I believe that's the fastest I ever saw Margret run, in my entire life. Yes indeed, Mama was upset over that for a good little while. But, after all the dust had settled Margaret, and I had learned some important lessons.

Overall, my siblings and I all got along well. Besides, Mama and Daddy would not tolerate us fussing and fighting all the time, anyway. And, of course, not having much, we all had to help one another and share with each other. Even at night, we had to share the same bed because we didn't have the luxury of sleeping in separate rooms and beds. My two sisters, my brother and I, all slept together on a lumpy corn husk-filled mattress. Though we began our slumber cuddled up in a spot of our own, we quickly became tangled as we shifted throughout the night. On those chilly nights, to keep warm we'd cuddle up together, underneath a thick quilt that Mama had made for us.

While fast asleep sometimes we'd be awakened by the presence of rats that crept into our room. The rats often scavenged around, at night, looking to eat the corn husks that were in our mattress. Occasionally, even snakes would make their way into our room through the holes that were in our bedroom floor. On one moonlit night, I just happened to wake up and see the shadowy figure of a snake slithering near the foot of our mattress. Overcome with fear, I screamed at the top of my lungs, startling everyone in the house. To this day, I'm still scared of those old ugly snakes. Every time I see a snake it reminds me of the devil. But by and by, we had a sound sleep and were never harmed by the wildlife typically found out in the country. All of those years growing up in that raggedy old house, it was the Lord that kept us from dangers both seen and unseen.

In the years that I grew up on that old farm, I guess most of the summers were all the same. The only thing that seemed to change was the hot relentless sun seemed to get hotter as the years went by. Though the summers in the country could be oh so beautiful, the same heaven could also rain down its fury in some terrible thunderstorms. Whenever it would rain, Mama rushed to place pots and pans underneath the leaks in our deteriorating roof. Usually, there were not enough pots and pans to go around catching all the rain that poured into our house.

One afternoon in June 1945, there was a terrible thunderstorm, the likes of which I'll never forget. In the distance, you could see the black thunderhead clouds massing and drawing closer to our farm. Suddenly the wind began to blow fiercely, and the temperature dropped sharply. Lightning streaked across the blackened sky as the thunder rolled and peeled above us. Bad storms have always been unnerving to me. It was like God was angry with us. However, this particular storm was a real humdinger. There were very strong wind gusts that were accompanied by torrents of rain. Our little house was so old and weakened that it offered us little refuge. Mama and Daddy quickly got us out of the house, and we all huddled outside underneath a blanket.

Although we had a storm cellar, we opted for being outside because all sorts of snakes and vermin were down in that dark musty old storm cellar. So there we were, all huddled together underneath the drenched blanket, when all of a sudden in the distance, we heard a loud explosion.

"What in the world was that?" Mama excitedly asked.

At first, we all thought it was more thunder, but after Daddy peeked his head out from underneath the blanket and looked in the direction of our neighbor's farm, he was astonished. Something was terribly wrong. Daddy just stood there with his mouth gaping wide open. Curiously, as we looked on we saw an ominous column of black smoke billowing up from the Jones' farm. Though none of us knew what had happened, one thing was for certain, a terrible fire was raging over there. But what could have been burning? Everything was soaking wet from the storm.

Then Daddy said, "Come on, let's go. The Jones' may need our help."

So Daddy hurried and got the wagon and we made haste as we rushed to our neighbor's aid. However, none of us would be prepared for what we would find just a quarter mile down the road. As we drew closer to our neighbor's farm, we discovered what had happened. There had been an awful plane crash.

In all my life, I have never seen anything like this. The scene was horrifically gory. There were parts of the aircraft that were scattered all over the Jones' farm. There were dismembered body parts and pools of blood. The terrible stench of burnt human flesh filled the noonday air. The noxious fumes from the burning fuel and metal made it difficult to breathe. The screams of the survivors crying out for help could be heard amongst the commotion of the burning airplane wreckage. This was all too overwhelming for me and I began to scream hysterically. Though Daddy quickly took me back home, it was too late because the images of this tragedy were already burned into my mind.

Since we were the only other family this side of Bear Creek, Daddy returned to help Mr. Jones in the rescue operations. Fortunately, the Jones' were one of the few families in the whole county that had a telephone, so they were able to call the authorities in Vicksburg. However, Vicksburg officials were not prepared for such a tragic accident either. Some even said that it was the worst tragedy in these parts since the Civil War. Unfortunately, there was only one ambulance available to transport the injured. Those who had died, their bodies remained at the crash site until the coroner could transport them to the county morgue.

To complicate matters even further, the heavy rains caused Bear Creek to overflow. Now that the banks of the creek had overflowed, the road to Vicksburg was cut off. Consequently, the emergency vehicles could not reach the crash site. Though there was an iron bridge that crossed over the creek, this creaky old bridge of Civil War vintage was in disrepair and no one trusted it. Therefore, the rescuers had to use boats to get across the creek to perform their rescue and recovery operations.

Due to the lack of emergency equipment, the rescuers made stretchers out of anything that they could. My daddy lent a helping hand by first using his wagon to transport the injured to the banks of Bear Creek. From there, others ferried them across by boat to vehicles waiting on the other side. After all the injured had been rescued, they began the grisly task of recovering the dead.

As my father would tell us later, some passengers could not be identified, because they had been either mangled or burned beyond recognition. Still, others were cut in half, decapitated and others lost limbs and bled to death. Pools of blood had mixed together with the wet muddy ground. Mud and blood were everywhere. Daddy had worked late into the night transporting the injured and the dead and after it was all over, he finally came home. As he stepped up unto the porch, you could hear the squishing sounds that his boots made. Daddy's clothes were soaked in blood. As soon as Daddy reached out to open the screen door to come into the house, I remember Mama yelling, "Stop! Don't you come in my house with dead men's blood!"

We were all shocked. We had never heard Mama yell at Daddy like that before. And considering that we were all a little superstitious, Mama wasn't about to let him into the house until he was cleansed from all the blood and the smell of death. My poor daddy, a gruesome sight to see, frustrated and fatigued didn't take another step, but turned back around and removed those bloody clothes just as mother insisted.

After Daddy cleaned himself up, Mama finally lets him back in the house. Daddy came in, sat down and uttered not a word, but the look on his face told the story of a man who looked like he had been to hell and back. Sadly, after all that terrible work Daddy did for the authorities that day, he was paid a measly ten dollars. This was hardly compensation for the morbid task my father performed.

As long as I live I'll never forget that day. This whole ordeal was a traumatic and a terrible emotional drain on us all. There were many nights that I didn't sleep well at all. The gory images of the crash site caused me to have horrifying nightmares. Frequently, I woke up screaming in the middle of the night. I was too afraid to go back to sleep because those terrible reoccurring nightmares might have continued. Mama would have to get up and console me. Sometimes she would let me come to lay down with her and Daddy until I went back to sleep.

As the time moved on, Mama and Daddy recovered quickly from the tragedy, but long after the wreckage was cleared away, the horrors of that afternoon lurked on in the recesses of my mind. Images of the crash frequently flickered before my eyes. Being the imaginative child that I was, I thought because I saw their bodies, the ghost of those killed in the crash would come to haunt me. Therefore, I had become even more afraid of the night and equally afraid to fall asleep. It took me a long time to completely get over this awful tragedy, but as the weeks and months rolled by, I too, moved on from the events of that horrible afternoon.

Although our family survived the storm of June 1945, it was truly unfortunate for the men that died on that ill-fated military flight. Some blamed the accident on the violent turbulence. Others said wind shear could have been the culprit of this terrible crash. In any event, whatever cause, one thing was certain, at least fifteen active duty and retired soldiers perished. As for me, the brutality of death became all too real on that somber summer day when life's innocence was lost forever.

Since it was the Lord who was so faithful in protecting and providing for us, Mama and Daddy felt obligated to show God our gratitude. So that meant Sundays were the Lord's Day, and we made it our priority to give thanks to God. Each Sunday morning, Mama would get us up early so we could get ready. After we had all eaten, Daddy would get the horses hitched up and the wagon ready to take us to the town of Bear Creek. That's where we attended the China Grove Baptist Church. The fifteen-mile ride was very rugged because the dirt roads were bumpy and full of holes, but that didn't stop Daddy from driving those old horses as fast as they could go. Daddy didn't ever want to be late for church which started at 11 a.m. sharp. Since the trip was so long, most of the time when we got there church had already started. As we drew closer to our little country church, we could hear the sounds of a jubilant congregation blaring out through the opened stained-glass windows. The piano would be playing, the choir singing, and the congregation clapping their hands while singing those uplifting hymns. Even as a little girl, I loved those old Negro spirituals that we sang during the worship services. And as it is to this day, I still love to praise the Lord. Intermittently, in the background, you could hear people shouting "Hallelujah, Praise the Lord!"

You could also hear the voice of Reverend George Lewis, pastor of China Grove Baptist Church, shouting, "Amen, Amen!"

Pastor Lewis had such a resonant baritone voice. It seemed to go right through you. Boy, he could really preach under the anointing of the Holy Ghost. Though China Grove only had eighty or so members, Pastor would preach as if though he was preaching to thousands of people in one of those huge cathedrals.

Between my sisters and my brother, I believe I enjoyed church the most. I say that because I would be paying more attention to the message than some of the other kids did. My older sister Margaret recalled one particular time when I prayed over the Sunday School class. As I understand it, it was quite some prayer because I tried to recite the whole Bible in the process.

After church service was over and everyone said their goodbyes,

Daddy got us all loaded up in the wagon for the long journey home. Being truly blessed and revived by the uplifting service, we sang songs of praise and worship as we made our way back to the farm.

Yes, these were truly wonderful times and are great memories of my younger years. The wagon rides I took with my family on those bumpy dirt roads. The long walk through the woods to school each day. Mama's home cooking on that wood-burning stove, and our little old farmhouse are all precious memories of a time when life was so simple. In the many nights that I slept on that crowded corn husk mattress, I could have never dreamed that I could come so far in life. I could never have imagined the years that I spent growing up on that farm would just be one of many stops on a long journey to a place where God was leading me.

Yes, there would be tougher roads to travel and longer journeys to take, along with trials, tribulations, victories, and successes. Just like the rest of us, I too, have often wondered, why do we have to travel the roads that we do in this life? What's the purpose in all the pain that we must endure? Yes, these are the questions I'm sure all of us have asked at one time or another. Yet as the Bible tells us, The steps of a good man are ordered by the LORD: and he delights in his way. Though he might fall, he shall not be cast down: for the LORD upholds him with his hand.[2] One thing is for sure, God knows what he's doing. He is the potter; we are the clay, therefore; He shapes us according to His plans and purpose for our lives. I really thank God for that.

# Chapter 2

## The Years in Vicksburg
## From the Country to the City

After many years had come and gone, the time had come for us to move away from the life that we once knew. Far from the rural trappings of our farm and away from the country trails that weaved through the backwoods of Warren County, far from that old Bear Creek that so often overflowed its banks. We were leaving the only place I have ever called home. Once we started packing none of us realized how much we had accumulated in such a small house. There was so much stuff that we couldn't take it all. There were some sentimental things that I just wanted for keepsakes, but we could only take the things we actually needed.

With our wagon loaded to capacity, we anxiously pulled away leaving the old behind and looking forward to the new. As I gazed back at that old farmhouse, it seemed to just drift away into the dusty distance. Also slipping away were the years that we had spent living, learning and laboring on that old farm. Our daily experiences there in Warren County would soon become relics of our past, tucked away in the recesses of our minds. Yet with great expectation, we wondered what we would find at the end of the thirty-five-mile ride to Vicksburg. This journey seemed to take an eternity, just as if we had traveled from one world to another. Though change doesn't come easy, this time there was an air of anticipation and excitement. As the old saying goes, the more things change, the more they stay the same. I would certainly find out that old saying was true, in the days, months and years to come, growing up in Vicksburg Mississippi.

When we arrived in Vicksburg, I immediately noticed that there was no comparison, between Warren County and the city. Vicksburg was densely populated and much more congested than Warren County. There were sidewalks and storefronts. There were tall streetlights that rose high above the paved streets. There were automobiles and traffic signs. There were shoppers that paced in and out of the many stores that ran along Main Street. Many of the buildings were made of solid brick and some stood taller than the pine trees that were back in Warren County. It was so much different than what I was used too. Everything seemed to be moving so much faster as if though everyone was in a big hurry. All of the commotion and hustle and bustle was a little overwhelming. Yet, the city was thrilling because it had such an irresistible air of excitement. There was so much going on and a lot to capture your attention.

As we made our way through downtown Vicksburg, I was really anxious to see our new house. Up until that moment, I had only heard Mama and Daddy talking about it. Along the way we saw so many fine houses, I wondered if ours was like some of those we were passing by. I couldn't wait to see it.

Finally, we turned onto the street where our new house was located. And for the very first time, I saw the street sign that rose high above the street. On the sign it was written, Grove Street. At last, we had arrived in our new neighborhood. There were many houses on our block and, a few of them had shiny automobiles parked out front. There were kids playing outside. The girls were jumping rope and playing hopscotch while the boys were running about playing ball and riding their bicycles. When our new neighbors saw us coming, they all seemed to pause for a moment. Their heads turned and their eyes followed us, as if, we were passing them in review. Curiously, they all watched as our wagon filled with our belongings stopped in front of our new home.

"This is it. We're here," Daddy said.

And for the first time, I'd laid eyes on our new house. Initially, I didn't move a muscle, but sat right there in my seat, giving the front of the house a good looking over. It was a beige house with brown trim. It also had a front yard and a porch with a swing. I thought, what a beautiful home. This is a dream come true. After pausing for a minute, I jumped down from the wagon. As I made my way to the walkway that led to our porch, I noticed our mailbox that was nestled atop a wooden pole. On its side was written, 1016 Grove Street. I then scurried up to the front door and went in right behind Mama. After entering, I stopped for a moment and began looking around. Wow! I was truly amazed. I had never set foot in such a fine house.

Our new house had a beautiful living room and dining room. Both rooms had shiny pinewood floors. The walls had been recently painted, so they were clean and white. There was a beautiful kitchen with formica counter tops, plenty of cabinet space and a gas burning stove as well. Our new home also had the modern conveniences of running water and electric lights. The only thing we still didn't have was a bathroom, however, there was an outhouse which was located in the backyard. Off behind the dining room, were two bedrooms. The master bedroom for Mama and Daddy and the smaller bedroom was for us kids. Just as it was in the country, the kids had to share a room, but this time Daddy had bought us some bunk beds to sleep in.

Yes, all the new surroundings took time to get used to. For instance, back in Warren County our nearest neighbors lived a mile down the road. But here in Vicksburg I could look right out of my bedroom window and see our next-door neighbor's house, right across our yard.

After the first few weeks had passed by, I knew all my neighbors by name, and I quickly made many new friends. This was so much better than the country because back in Warren County we lived so far away from one another. The only time we really saw other kids were on the days that we went to school, but here in Vicksburg, there were plenty of kids our age to socialize with.

Another advantage of our new neighborhood was the corner store right down the street from our house. I used to love to go down to the store. Most of the time instead of buying candy; I really went down there to meet up with my new girlfriends. Being the naïve little country girl that I was, I wanted to fit it with the neighborhood girls. Therefore, it wasn't long before I got in the clique with the fast girls. Most of the time we would wait for the boys to show up. We used to make eyes and giggle at them as they would pass us by. I guess we were acting like the silly girls that we were. Yet slowly but surely, I was being converted to the ways of the promiscuous neighborhood girls. So as the days, weeks and months went by, my interest was quickly turning from toys to boys.

My fourteenth birthday had come and gone and I had begun to mature rapidly. My body had begun to develop in the most feminine way. Now that I was becoming a beautiful young lady, the boys were really starting to notice me and I started to notice them too. It was the summer of 1948, everything around me and in me, seemed to be coming alive. It was like there was another person inside me that wanted to bust out and engage my curiosities and desires. At the time it seemed like there was nothing more important to me than being with my girlfriends. I tried so hard to fit in and to be accepted. Yet, like the other girls my age, I was hard-headed. I wanted to be grown. Soon that way of thinking would take its toll on me. As the old saying goes the chickens would soon come home to roost.

As the summer of 1948 was coming to a close and the new school semester was about to begin, I attended my first year of school there at Magnolia Junior High School. Magnolia Junior High was located on the other side of town, a few miles away from our neighborhood. The building still remains to this day, right there on Cherry Street. I'll never forget the day I stepped foot inside that school. Magnolia Junior High was far different from the one-room schoolhouse back in Warren County. This huge three-story building was the largest building I had ever seen.

Inside, were long hallways with bright shiny tile floors. There were lockers that lined the hallways and there were many classrooms. I can remember thinking, I'll never learn my way around this big old school. I'll get lost, going from one class to the next. Inside the classrooms, were thirty or so of those old fashion student's desks. They were all lined up in straight rows that ran about the length of the classroom. At the head of the classroom, was the large teacher's desk. Behind it were the blackboards where the teacher wrote out our lessons. Sometimes while writing on the blackboard, the chalk would make that eerie screeching sound that sent chills up your spine. I used to hate it when the chalk used to make that sound.

There were also large windowpanes that lined one of the classroom walls, making way for plenty of daylight to enter. Whenever the sun was too bright, the teacher had a long wooden pole with a hook on the end, to pull down the window shades. My seat was right by the window. Being easily distracted, I spent more time daydreaming and gazing out the window, than I did paying attention to the lesson.

At Magnolia High, there were also other big differences. For example, for each class, there was a different classroom and each class period lasted about forty-five minutes. When the classes were over, the bells would ring aloud to indicate that the class period was over. I was startled the first time I heard those loud school bells ring. When the period was over, the students dashed out of the classrooms like racehorses darting out of a starting gate. Everyone was in a big hurry to get to their next class before the bells rang again. Then once again, the bells would ring and in an instant, the hallways would be cleared and quiet. At that point, all you could hear was the sound of doors shutting as the last students hurried into their classrooms. Boy oh boy, education city style involved so much more. It was no comparison to the primitive simplicity of the one-room schoolhouse back in the country. Yes, with all of this change, going to school had taken on a whole new light.

However, some things hadn't changed. Daddy was still a farmer and during planting and harvesting season, we continued to go to the cotton fields. That meant that we had to miss a lot of school days during the semester which kept us behind in our studies. I was so embarrassed. My friends had passed on to the next grades, but I was going on fifteen and still only in the seventh grade. However, I wasn't the only student behind because they had to work the cotton fields. Back in those days, it wasn't uncommon for kids to be absent from school during certain times of the year.

While at Magnolia Junior High, I made many more new friends. We had so much fun. Occasionally, I could attend some social gatherings that took place at the school. We called them sock-hops, where the school kids could dance to the popular music and socialize. My parents didn't approve of the music that I had begun to like. They referred to it as the Blues. I can remember daddy saying, "Music like that is unfit for Christians to be listening to."

Not to even mention all that close-up dancing we did. Well, music, dancing and having a good time, became the forbidden fruit that I just had to have. At this stage of life, I had a mind of my own and being obedient to my parents' dictates was not the highest item on my list of priorities.

There was no doubt about it, I was being influenced by all the hip kids at Magnolia High. I didn't want to come off as being a square. Like other teenage girls, I wanted to be popular with the guys. So my girlfriend introduced me to a suave young man who I'll call Percy Jones (fictional name). Percy was my first love. He was a couple years older than I and had already finished high school. I'm telling you the truth, I really fell head over heels for him. He was so fine. He was tall and fair skinned with wavy black hair that was always trimmed and neat. Percy wasn't like a lot of your average teenage boys who were interested in me. He was so mature, and he often spoke of the big dreams he had for his future. Percy really gave me the impression of someone who was going places in life. Besides that, he had all the fine material things that a young woman would really be excited about. He dressed well and drove a fine automobile. He also kept money in his pockets because he had a steady job. Last but not least, he had a charming personality with a good sense of humor. All these wonderful characteristics made him simply irresistible.

Right from the start, I had my eyes on Percy and he had his eyes on me. Whenever we were together, there was such an air of romantic bliss. Like me, Percy loved music, and he even played the guitar in a local band. Whenever I got the chance, I would go to see him play his guitar. But most of the time, I would just like to spend time with him at his place. I cherished the moments that we could be alone together. On many evenings we danced cheek-to-cheek to soft romantic music.

It wasn't long after our many romantic interludes that I was struck by one of Cupid's arrows and I fell deeply in love with Percy. With much passion and desire between us, nature soon took its course and at the age of seventeen, I became pregnant with Percy's first child. Her name was Elizabeth.

Percy took the news that he was going to be a father well, but Daddy didn't take the news he was going to be a grandfather very well at all. You see, since we were raised up in church, to Mama and Daddy, it was a shameful thing to be an unwed woman with babies. Especially back in those days, everyone frowned on a woman with illegitimate children. Well, at that point, Mama and Daddy tried their best to keep Percy and me from seeing each other, but it didn't work. At the same time, Mama knew I was too young to try to raise a baby by myself, so she helped care for Elizabeth. I loved my baby girl so much and I refused to consider this precious gift as illegitimate. How can a human being be illegitimate when each one of us is a unique soul and precious in the sight of God?

Since I had to support my daughter eventually I dropped out of school and got a job at the Holiday Inn in downtown Vicksburg. About a year after having my first child, I was pregnant with Percy's second child. Her name was Selestine. Well, that was the last straw. Mama and Daddy were both furious and they told me that I had to leave home. Fortunately, since I was working, Percy, and I got a larger apartment and we moved in together.

For the first time in life, I felt the agonizing pain of being rejected by my own family. I was deeply hurt and cried bitterly, but to make matters even worse, my so-called friends all laughed at me and I became the talk among all of my friends and associates. They said terrible things like she's eighteen years old, a baby in one hand and another one on the way with no husband. This experience taught me how quickly people will abandon you when the chips are down.

It seemed as if though I didn't have a friend in the world. However, during this time, I met a really nice young lady named Jo Ann (fictional name). She was kind and understanding and didn't seem to care so much about the predicament I was in. She was really down to earth and supportive, so we became the best of friends.

Not long afterward, I became pregnant with Percy's third child, Barbara Ann. By this time, the novelty had worn off. Percy, the man that I loved so much, the man that had dreams to fulfill and goals to accomplish, the man that had it all together, had no desire being tied down to me and the three children he fathered.

I remember him saying, "Louise, you're just too fertile for me. I don't want to spend the rest of my life stuck in a house full of babies." With that, Percy soon left me, and it absolutely crushed me. Being abandoned by the man I loved hurt worse than when my mother and father rejected me. At least when my parents told me to leave, I had Percy to turn to. But when Percy left me I had no one to turn to. I didn't know what I was going to do. In order to have my baby, I would have to take off months from my job. How was I going to keep my apartment? I was desperate and afraid. For the first time in my life, I was standing alone, with two mouths to feed and another on the way.

Although I was afraid, I was still determined to make it. I had to be. For the sake of my children, I had to survive. To add insult to injury, I found out that Percy was having an affair with my best friend Jo Ann. The very one who seemed to be so loving and caring stole my man from me. As blind as I was, I suspected nothing between them, but when I heard about it, I was devastated and felt like the biggest fool on God's green earth. It was so much pain to bear. I guess just like any woman that has been hurt by a man, I said, I'll never fall in love again. Yet I knew all along, my desires for a man were still very strong. I longed to love and longed to be in love. Even a broken heart will give way to passion, eventually.

In retrospect, I guess the reason why I fell in love with Percy is that I was hungry for attention and excitement. I was living in the city and experiencing new things. I was young and energetic, yet gullible to Percy's irresistible charm. Percy was that excitement that I was searching for. He was like the rhythm that caused the passions of my heart to beat. He was going places that I wanted to go. Percy was the safety and security I thought I needed oh so badly.

# Love and Charity

I didn't realize it at the time, but I was trying to fill a void in my life. Oh, how I wanted a warm, compassionate man in my life. Though Daddy was strong and supportive, he wasn't very emotional, though I know he loved me. Unfortunately, he rarely hugged and embraced me. We didn't have the heart-to-heart father-daughter talks. No, Daddy was always working so hard to keep a roof over our heads, but in the process, my heart was left exposed.

Therefore, Percy became the man that I could look up to. Women often use their father's characteristics, as a way to measure a prospective mate. Since Percy was hardworking and determined, I really believed that he was the man for me. I guess there's a little girl in every woman's heart desiring to be loved and cared for by the right man, and most likely a man similar to her father.

So there I was, needing to be needed, and wanting to be wanted, but I made the terrible mistake of confusing lust with love. We were simply unprepared for the realities that an intimate relationship brings. Nor did either one of us have the slightest idea of the level of commitment required in a healthy, loving relationship. Being young and restless, I made choices that would have an impact on the rest of my life.

Many years have come and gone since I've last seen Percy. Though he hurt me, the passing time has a way of healing old wounds. Besides, in God's plans, there are no mistakes. God knows our beginning and our ending and he has a wonderful way of making everything, work out for our good. I hear Percy did well and accomplished big things in his life. Obviously, he must have learned from his mistakes as well. As I understand it, Percy was a city official in Vicksburg for many years.

As the old saying goes, "Behind every dark cloud, there's a silver lining." Well, after all the dark clouds that had been hovering over my life, it was high time for me to experience one of those silver linings.

Little did I know the hand of the Lord would intervene and alter the course of my life. And from that point on, my life would never be the same.

After I had my third child, I was home in my apartment, getting back into my daily routine, when there came a knock at the door. I opened it, and there stood an elderly white woman, dressed all in white. She identified herself as a nurse sent over by the Department of Health. Back in those days the Department of Health, often sent nurses to check on the new mothers, to see if they needed any assistance or any postnatal care. Well, I invited her in, and she asked me the routine questions and checked to see if everything was all right. After she finished examining my newborn baby, she looked over to my other two children. And then she looked back at me and began to shake her head. Something was terribly wrong. She disapproved of something.

She then looked me in the eye, and said, "You have sinned a great sin, and you must give your life over to Jesus! God is not happy with you, having all these illegitimate babies!"

Well, I was shocked and I didn't know what to say, but I do remember, I felt so bad. It was awful. Then this austere woman lifted up her head and hands, looking up as though she was looking into heaven itself. And she began to pray and intercede on my behalf. I remember the words of her mighty prayer as though it happened yesterday.

She said, "Lord, give this woman a mind to stop sinning, and let her see how she has hurt you by having all these babies. Give her a mind to repent and change her evil ways."

Well, as long as I live, I'll never forget that day when that woman prayed for me. All I can remember was my heart was pricked, and a heavy spirit of conviction came over me. As I cradled my newborn baby in my arms, I dropped to my knees, and I began to weep from the very pit of my heart. As I looked up to heaven with tears streaming down my face, I asked the Lord Jesus to forgive me for my many sins. And while there on my knees I cried out to Jesus, asking him to give me a companion, someone who would love me and care for my little children.

After pouring myself out onto the Lord, my heart I felt so much better. It was just as the old Spiritual Hymn says, "Heaven came down and Glory filled my soul." A great peace came over me, and I knew God had heard my prayer. Deep down on the inside, I had a feeling that everything was gonna be all right. Yes, I knew, someway somehow, that Jesus was gonna work it out. This was a great moment in my life, and a turning point as well.

Yes, the Lord had surely visited me that day, and it all began with that nurse knocking at my door. Just like it says in the Bible, "Behold I stand at the door and knock, If anyone hears My voice and opens the door, I will come into him and sup with him and he with me."3 The Lord truly sent his messenger to me that day. That old praying woman, just like an angel, brought words from heaven to speak encouragement into my heart. It's funny after that old white woman left my apartment, I would never see her face again. Sometimes, God places people in your life, not to establish ongoing relationships, but as a signpost that points you in the direction that He wants you to go.

As the months passed by, harvest season was now upon us once again. Since economic times were still hard, many of us continued to pick cotton to earn extra money. So every morning a truck would come around about four a.m., to take us to the various farms to work. After we took our place on the truck, we'd be on our way to the cotton fields. It was a ride I took any number of mornings during harvest season. It was all quite predictable, nothing new, except for this one particular morning things would turn out to be quite different.

As the starlit sky slowly gave way to the rising sun, the love songs of the robins drifted through the warm summer breeze. I was just sitting there daydreaming, not paying any particular attention to anyone, I looked up and caught a pair of big delightful eyes peering right into mine. They belonged to a handsome young man, who was sitting right across from me. At first, he suddenly looked away, because I had caught him staring, but he couldn't take his eyes off of me. He just kept on looking at me. At first, I pretended not to notice him, but soon his glances turned to a smile. The smile led to a hello, and then he introduced himself to me. His name was James Hunter.

Mr. James Hunter had the biggest, dreamy eyes that I had ever seen. I could tell he had something on his mind. It was all in the way that he was looking at me. His smile was a subtle invitation to get to know me. My intuition was quickly able to discern that James was certainly interested in me. However, I let on like I wasn't interested in him. But I was really charmed out of my shoes. It felt so good having an admirer. So I stopped pretending I wasn't interested and I engaged him in conversation. And after we introduced ourselves, it wasn't long before we became acquainted with one another.

As the days and weeks went by, I looked forward to seeing James on the truck in the mornings. We would talk all the way to the cotton fields. I must have talked this poor man's ears off, but he didn't mind because he was a good listener. I told him about the many things that I had gone through, and about some problems that I had been having. I must admit, I was hesitant to tell him about my three children right away. I didn't want to scare him off. After all, it wasn't the most socially acceptable thing to be an unwed mother back in the '50s, but my having children didn't seem to bother James at all. As a matter of fact, he wanted to meet them, so I invited James over for dinner and he readily accepted my invitation.

On a warm Saturday afternoon and I prepared some of my delicious fried chicken. I told the girls that a guest would be joining us for dinner and that they should be on their best behavior. James arrived on time, and I introduced him to my daughters. James really interacted well with them, and the children really enjoy him. I was so happy. This was an answer to prayer. I'd found a man that cared for my children and was unfazed by my predicament. James wanted me for just who I was. As time went on, our hearts grew fond of one another and once again I was falling in love. On a warm summer day, James and I were taking a walk through a lovely park there in Vicksburg. We were enjoying one another's company and discussing our future. After walking for a while we sat down on a park bench, right under a big oak tree. James then knelt down on one knee and removed his hat. He gently held my hands and looked at me with those big dreamy eyes of his.

He then asked me, "Louise, will you marry me?"

I was totally shocked. James' proposal took me by surprise. This was the first time that someone had formally proposed to me. "Yes, James, I'll marry you," I replied.

We then held each other in a passionate embrace. It was all so romantic. A few days later we went to the Justice of the Peace and got married. After knowing James Hunter for only about three months, he was now my husband, and I was now, Mrs. Louise Hunter.

Being married was great. It was like a big weight had been lifted off my shoulders. Now my heart was pleasantly relieved. I was like a damsel in distress and then came James Hunter like a knight in shining armor to rescue me. A new and wonderful chapter had been opened in my life. At last, I'm validated. I'm now both a proud mother and a wife. I don't have to hang my head low in shame any longer. I'm Louise Hunter and I'm proud of it! For the first time in a long time, I felt good about myself. I had enough confidence to take on the world. I was no longer ashamed of what all the gossipers were saying. Surely Mama and Daddy would no longer have to be ashamed of me. At last, they could accept me and rest assured that I had finally done the right thing. Now that I was married, from time to time, I thought about the day that the nurse came to my apartment. I remembered how I cried out to the Lord and asked him to give me a companion. When James came into my life, I knew for sure that there was nothing that was too hard for God. I learned that though there might be times where God seems far away and disinterested in the situations in our lives, this really isn't true. God always wants what's best for us, even when we don't understand His ways, he still has our best interests in mind. Yes, indeed, only the Lord could have lifted me out of that horrible pit of shame that I was in. And He did it by blessing me with such a wonderful man as James Hunter.

# Chapter 3
## The Trials of Marriage

During the early year of our marriage, James and I went through the normal period of adjustment. James rented a small apartment that all five of us squeezed into. Though we didn't have much, overall we were happy with one another. Just as any good man, James had high hopes for his new family, but he didn't have the means or the finances to make those dreams come true. Though things cost a lot less back in those days, the wages were also much lower, therefore; it was still a struggle to make ends meet. But just as James was determined to be a good husband and provider, I was determined to be a good wife and mother. This meant that my focus was on giving James his first child. And with that in mind, it wasn't long before my desires to get pregnant came to pass. Soon James and I had our first baby boy. His name was James Junior (2014).

Since the job that James had didn't pay enough money, James was always looking for extra work to help make ends meet. Getting by the best we could, James finally got a job picking tobacco in Kinson, North Carolina. He would go there once a year and stay during the entire harvest season. The idea of being separated from James didn't sit well with me. However, James faithfully sent money back from Kinson. When harvest season was over, he always returned home to us.

After a few harvests had come and gone, James was ready to move us all to Kinson. All while James had been going to Kinson, he was busy staking his claim there, so he could move our family there permanently. While in Kinson, James was able to land one of those jobs working for the city. Everyone wanted one of those civil service jobs because they paid well and offered good benefits. He had also gotten us a nice three-bedroom apartment and was ready for us to move to Kinson with him. So we packed up all our possessions and moved away to Kinson, North Carolina.

When I got to Kinson, I really liked it. Like Vicksburg, it was a city with things to do and places to go, but life was better here in Kinson than it was back in Vicksburg. James was making good money now, and the bills were getting paid. Finally, our situation was improving, but not everything was changing for the better. Soon, James and I had become sidetracked by the pursuit of good times and the nightlife. By this time James and I had two children, James Junior and Zoline. But once I got a taste of Kinson's nightlife, I didn't want to be stuck in the house with the kids all day. I wanted to get out and party and live it up some. So I did just that, and James was right there along with me, but little did I know at the time, the Hunter family was headed for some serious trouble. Since James and I were so busy having a good time, we were too blind to see the rocky shores that we were slowly drifting toward.

It's funny how quickly we forget where we come from. Yes, how soon I had forgotten the day that I cried out to the Lord, and asked him to forgive my sins. I had forgotten that I gave my life to Him back in Vicksburg. Now that I was in a new place, it was like I didn't know who the Lord was anymore. I must have thought I'd moved far enough away for Him not to see the life I had started living. In the midst of seeking the pleasures of sin there in Kinson, time passed quickly, and a year had come and gone.

One day I was at home in the apartment and there came a knock at the door. I opened it and there stood a stranger. It was an elderly black woman clothed in a long white dress and she wore a white cloth, wrapped around her head like a turban. From her neck hung a large golden cross.

"May I help you?" I asked.

She hastily replied, "The Lord sent me here. I must come in and pray for you."

Well, I was enjoying life just as it was, and I wasn't about to do no changing. I didn't want to hear what she had to say, so I refused her. "No that's all right," I insisted.

But then she began to plead with me, saying, "Please let me in. I must pray for you now," she insisted. Then she said something that really got my attention. She said, "You promised God something! If you don't come back to God, a tragedy is on its way!"

As soon as she said this, I instantly remembered the nurse back in Vicksburg, but I shrugged this off as a mere coincidence, and in unbelief, I slammed the door in her face. I thought, *Ain't that something? Some weird old lady, out of nowhere, just coming to my door like that. There are some strange people out here in Kinson, North Carolina.* Yes, these were my unfortunate thoughts concerning this situation. Yet, it disturbed me. How could she have known about the promise I made to God back in Vicksburg years ago? Nevertheless, I dismissed all with a nervous, "Oh well" and then went on about my business there in the apartment.

Two days had come and gone since the stranger had visited us. On the morning of the third day, I got up and fed the kids. James was already gone to work. I remember having to comb my youngest daughter Zoline's hair. Boy, that child just put up a fuss and wouldn't sit still for anything. Zo, as I call her, had some long, pretty black hair. Like the rest of my daughters, she was such a beautiful little girl. Well, after I was finished tending to the children, I decided to leave home for a while and go out with some of my girlfriends. *The kids will be all right*, I thought. *I'll just be gone a little while,* so off I went not realizing that the strange woman's prophecy was about to come true.

I was on my way back home after being gone for a few hours. As I was drawing closer to my apartment building, in the distance, I could see that there were fire trucks in front of our building. I thought out loud, *What in the world is going on over there?*

But as I got closer to our apartment building, one of my neighbors ran up to me and said, "There has been a fire in your apartment, and one of your babies has been burned to death."

When I heard that, it was like I had been struck by a bolt of lightning. I was so shocked that my knees buckled. Then I totally panicked. I was completely hysterical. I grabbed my head, then went running down the street towards my apartment as fast as I could.

When I reached my building, one of the neighbors said, "They took your baby girl to the hospital."

"Zoline! My little baby Zoline!" I shouted.

Then in complete hysteria, I ran towards the hospital. It hadn't crossed my mind that the hospital was a couple of miles away. As I was running down the street at a desperate pace, a cab was passing by.

The cab stopped, and the driver asked me, "Lady, what's wrong?

Where are you going in such a hurry?"

I said, "Please take me to the hospital. My baby has been burned up in a fire."

The cab driver quickly obliged me, so I jumped into the cab. However, as soon as I got in the back seat of the cab, it was if I could hear a voice saying, "I warned you, and you would not hear!"

I then recalled the now prophetic words the lady had said to me just three days earlier. I remembered how she begged me to let her in to pray for me. I remembered how she warned me about this impending tragedy. While the cab whisked its way to the hospital, I was overcome with guilt. With my face down to my knees, I wept bitterly all the way to the hospital. Why didn't I listen? Why did I slam the door in her face? Why did I leave my precious little babies at home alone? I heard echoing throughout my grief-stricken conscience, time and time again.

A surge of desperation seemed to overcome me, so I yelled at the cab driver, "Please hurry! Is this as fast as you can go?"

Responding to my urgency, the cab driver sped up and began weaving in and out of traffic, honking his horn, at the other vehicles to get out of our way. Though it had only been minutes, it seemed like it took hours to reach the hospital. As soon as we arrived, I got out of the cab and was about to enter the hospital, and to my astonishment, that strange woman who predicted this tragedy was there at the hospital! I couldn't believe it. She was standing outside in front of the emergency room entrance. Ironically, she was wearing the same garb that she wore three days ago when she came to my apartment. *Oh no, not her again*, I thought aloud. Not wanting to face her, I hurried by as if I didn't know she was there.

Once in the hospital, I worked my way back to the emergency room. When I opened the emergency room door, I peeped in, and I saw my, little Zoline. My baby seemed to be covered in gauze and bandages from head to toe. Nurses and doctors hurriedly attended to her second and third-degree burns. Carefully, they removed pieces of charred skin as she just lay there limp and unconscious. I couldn't stand it.

My stomach was getting queasy, I felt as if I was going to be sick, so I turned away. I just couldn't bear to see my child laying there like that on the operating table. It was just too much for me. Now, afraid and confused, I was coming completely unglued. And all the time, I kept on hearing that same taunting voice, repeating over and over again, *"I warned you, but you would not hear!"*

Not knowing what to do, or knowing who to turn too, I ran to the nearest telephone to call my mother back in Vicksburg. I thought things would be all right if Mama would pray for me! But when I went to pick up the telephone and began to dial her number. The voice said, *"You pray, it's not your mother's responsibility, it's yours."*

My first thought was, *"I can't pray. God will not hear me."*

Then the voice again commanded, *"Pray."* And right there at the telephone booth, I fell down to my knees and I began to pray.

I said, "Lord, please allow me to have another chance. Lord, please don't take my child. I'll never let you down again," I pleaded and pleaded.

While I was kneeling down at the telephone booth, repenting and crying out to Jesus, I could feel the peace of God resting deep in my soul. So I stood to my feet and ran back to the emergency room. As I peered through the window, I saw her limp little body begin to twitch, and her head moved slightly. Right there before my very eyes, miraculously Zoline regained consciousness. God's healing virtue began to revive Zoline as she laid there on the operating table. So I went into the emergency room and told them who I was. "How is she?" I asked.

"Miss, I'll be honest with you I thought that this kid was in serious trouble. Her pulse and respirations were barely detectable, but all of a sudden, she started making a remarkable recovery. She's got some second and third-degree burns that we are concerned about but they'll heal in time. She seems to be a real fighter, I think she's gonna be all right," the doctor replied.

Although the doctors used the term, "recovery" I knew this was nothing short of a miracle.

When I turned my face to the Lord, He heard my prayer and delivered Zoline from death. And just as God had given her new life, he had also given me another chance in life. Yes, just as the Bible says about Jesus, that He will not leave you or forsake you. Once again the Lord had proven his faithfulness to me when I knew I didn't deserve it. He didn't have to do it, but He did. He may not have come when I wanted Him to, but He was right on time.

Looking back at it, the Lord taught me something in the midst of this tragedy, that I will never forget. The Lord said to me, *"You pray. It's your responsibility."* This was so true. It wasn't anyone else's responsibility but mine.

When I humbled myself and prayed, God Almighty moved and rebuked death off of my daughter. It's just like the Bible says, "If my people which are called by my name, would humble themselves and pray, and turn from their wicked ways; then shall I hear from heaven and heal their land."[4] Whether you're the preacher or the teacher, high or low, God is not a respecter of persons. It makes no difference in the eyesight of the Lord. If you will humble yourself and pray, God will move for you. This was something that I had to learn for myself. There isn't a textbook or a classroom where I could have learned what I did that day.

After the smoke of this tragedy cleared from our hearts and minds, we moved away from the tragic memories of this apartment. It took Zoline a full year to recover from her burns. Fortunately, she was only four years old when this happened. Her skin eventually healed and cleared up and her beautiful black hair slowly returned. While she was in and out of the hospital for most of that year, James got us an apartment in the housing projects there in Kinson. This whole ordeal weighed heavily on James' heart. Although Zoline was his second child, she was still Daddy's little girl.

Throughout that year James was compassionate and very supportive, but he still had his old worldly ways. As for me, I was finished with the nightlife for good, but James continued to step out at night. As time went on, James would go out more and more, hanging around with his old drinking buddies. James couldn't see it but none of his so-called friends meant him any good. Some of them weren't working; others had no wives or no real responsibilities. They were the kind of friends that no wife wants to see her husband associating with. However, James would continuously swear by them.

Though James never physically abused me, he was definitely changing for the worse. We had begun to argue, more and more, as he came home later and later at night, each time reeking with the smell of cheap whiskey. Since James' behavior continued like it did it wasn't long before he lost his city job. From there, things between us continued on a downward spiral.

Even though things weren't going well at home, I was certainly determined not to leave the Lord out of my life ever again. I had purposed in my heart that I was going to live right for the Lord no matter what. Although I'd seen some good days, and I'd seen some bad days, I wasn't going to complain, because Jesus has been too good to me.

Well, one Sunday evening, the kids and I were preparing to go to church, and I asked James to come along with us. James was being obstinate and refused to come along with us. However, I was not about to let his reluctance stop me from praising God, so off to church, the kids and I went. After the service was over, the joy of the Lord was in me. I was uplifted and my spirit had been revived. It had been a long day, and I was really tired, so shortly after returning home, I put the kids to bed and I turned in too.

The next morning when I woke up the bed was empty. James was gone. Apparently, he had tipped out sometime during the night as I slept. "Where has this man gone to now?" I asked myself.

I assumed that he'd gone down the street to one of his friends' houses or something, but then a mutual friend of ours stopped by the house, to tell me the bad news.

"Girl, James is gone," he said.

"James is not gone, nowhere. He's just probably down the street at one of his friends' somewhere," I replied.

And then he said, "No, Louise! James had his suitcases. He was heading for the Greyhound station."

So I ran into the bedroom to check the closet. It was true, all James' clothes were gone. I was absolutely devastated. Being abandoned once again, I fell across the bed and cried. I asked the Lord, "Lord Jesus, what am I going to do now?"

By this time I had seven little mouths to feed, and I was pregnant with my eighth child. James had left me high and dry, with no money, and not as much as a piece of bread to feed my hungry little children. At the point of desperation, I remembered what the Lord had told me at the hospital emergency room. The Lord told me, "You Pray," and pray I did. I told Jesus, *Lord, my kids don't have food to eat, and I don't know what I am going to do, but no matter what, I am determined to hold on to you, Lord.*

In answer to my prayer, the Lord brought back the memory of the woman that brought us the Christmas baskets last year.

"That's right!" I exclaimed.

After the fire, there was a woman who was kind to us last Christmas. She was being a Good Samaritan by donating some food and toys to us, but I didn't know how to get in contact with her. I didn't even know her name. Then I also remembered that she said she was a real estate agent and had an office on Main Street. Not being sure where I'd find this woman, I decided to walk down Main Street until I found her. So my seven babies and I all walked six blocks down Main Street until we finally found her office.

As soon as we walked into her office, she remembered who I was and I began to pour my heart out to her, telling her everything that had just happened to me.

After she heard me out, she said, "I understand."

Then I watched the Lord move in a mighty way. She got up from her desk and said, "Let's go."

We all got in her car and she drove us to the nearest grocery store. When we arrived there, she told me to get all the groceries that I needed. So after I practically filled up a shopping cart, she paid for it and then took us home. When we got back to my apartment, she told me that she would return in the morning to see if I needed anything else.

The next day came and she returned just as she said she would, and she asked me, if would I like to go back to Vicksburg, and I thought, *"Look at God!"*

I had just prayed and asked the Lord to make a way for us to go back home that very morning. I didn't want to have my baby all alone here in Kinson. I wanted to go back home to Vicksburg where I had some family. So I told her, "Yes, I would like to go back home."

So for the next two days, I packed up our belongings. And the following day she took us to the bus station and paid our fares back to Mississippi. I thank God for her. She certainly exemplifies what a Good Samaritan is.

After arriving in Vicksburg, I went to my mother's house and asked if she would put us up for a while. Understanding the predicament I was in, she didn't mind helping. Although I was four months' pregnant, I was still willing to work. I desperately needed money to care for my children. So I called my old job back and asked them would they please reconsider me for employment. My former boss said, "Sure, Louise, you were a good worker. It's all right for you to return."

I was glad that I hadn't burnt any bridges because I really needed to come back to this job.

Well, after I had gotten back into the swing of things, I began to search for James. I wasn't going to let him go that easily. Then, finally I got word that he was living in Natchez, Mississippi, so one weekend my father and I drove down to Natchez and sure enough, that's where we caught up with him.

James was completely astonished that I'd found him in Natchez. The first thing he said to me was, "What you doing here in Natchez? How did you make it back here from Kinson?"

Ooh! the nerve of that man asking me that, after he had abandoned us. But the Lord gave me the strength to keep my tongue.

So I told him, "I didn't do it, Jesus did it."

After hearing that he just stood there in silence with a stupid look on his face. He simply couldn't believe it. After that initial encounter with James in Natchez, we soon made up, and we agreed that we should get back together and return to Vicksburg.

Shortly after James returned to Vicksburg, he was also able to get his old job back. However, with both of us working, we were still struggling too hard there in Vicksburg.

So James and I were talking over our situation one night and he said, "I have a cousin up north in Wisconsin. Maybe if I call and ask her, she'll let us stay with her until we can get on our feet. I hear it's nice up there, and there's plenty of work up there too."

He called his cousin, and she agreed to let us stay with her. So once again we were making preparations to move, but this time we were heading up north to Wisconsin, to a small town named Racine.

# Chapter 4
## The Land of Promise and Pain

Once James and I received our first paychecks, we had enough money to make the move to Racine, Wisconsin. Somehow we thought a change of location would be the answer to our problems. However, as we would soon find out, getting a fresh start doesn't mean problems will go away. Troubles can be like clothes packed away inside a suitcase. Though they're tucked away out of sight during the journey, as soon as you arrive at your destination, you unpack them and wear them once again.

After a long day of preparations and packing, we were ready to leave for the bus station. This time we had decided only to take what we could get into the storage compartments on the bus. We left Vicksburg with just a little more than the clothes on our backs. We said our goodbyes to Mama and loaded up our belongings in Daddy's station wagon. As we road to the bus station, there was an uneasy silence in the car. Quietly we collected our thoughts as we anticipated the new life that awaited us in Racine. Shortly after arriving at the bus station, James got in line and purchased our tickets. We then said our goodbyes to Daddy, and we all embraced him.

"Y'all take care now, ya hear? Call us when you get there." Daddy requested.

"OK, Daddy," I replied as I boarded the bus.

After getting on the bus, we tucked our belongings away in the overhead racks and then took our seats. When I glanced out of the window Daddy was still standing there waiting to see us off. After the driver started the bus, moments later we pulled away. I looked back at Daddy and saw him waving goodbye as the bus moved on down the road. It had come to pass. We were finally leaving Mississippi, the old Magnolia state of the gallant South. Gone forever would be the red dirt, the tall pines, and the cotton fields of misery. Thus we began our long journey up north to Racine, Wisconsin.

The bus was crowded, and every seat was taken. It seemed like everybody in Vicksburg was on the bus that day. We were all packed in like sardines on that stuffy old bus. After the first few hours, our kids had become very restless.

"Mama, Are We There Yet? Mama, when we gonna get there?"

They must have asked me that a million times. They really started to get on my nerves, but I kept in mind that it's impossible for kids to sit still on a long trip. Besides, I was getting restless myself. There were also other mothers on the bus that had children as well. Some of these young mothers had infants which screamed and cried all the way to Racine. On top of all the noise, the seats were lumpy and very uncomfortable. As bad as I needed it, I didn't get much rest. During the entire eighteen-hour journey I don't believe I got a good solid hour of sleep. I just shifted in my seat, from one side to the other, trying to get as comfortable as possibly I could. That's how it was, hour after grueling hour. Fortunately, the bus made several stops along the way and we got a chance to stretch our legs a bit.

As we left St. Louis, the great Gateway Arch seemed to shrink away in the distance. Soon after, we crossed over the Mississippi River into Illinois and excitement began to build. "We'll be passing through the Windy City after while," James said with enthusiasm. By this time my imagination was running wild. I had heard so much about the

North, and I liked the idea that they didn't grow cotton up there. For the first time in my life, picking cotton during those hot summers in the Deep South was not an option. No, I don't think I'll be missing the south nor Mississippi any time soon.

After leaving the bus station in Chicago, the next stop was Racine. I was so glad that we were finally coming to the end of that long arduous journey. Boy, it seemed like that bus ride was taking forever. I must have counted each one of those long eighteen hours it took for us to reach our destination. As long as I live I never want to have to ride the bus for that long ever again.

As we were drawing closer to Racine, James really seemed to be getting anxious. He just kept saying, "You'll like my cousin, Louise, Yeah she's some kinda woman, you'll see."

And of course I believed him. What else was I going to do? We'd come too far now to turn back now. I remember how I prayed, "Lord God please make a way for us. We're coming to a strange town, a thousand miles away from home, but I trust that you will lead us in the right direction."

At last, we had finally arrived in Racine. After the bus came to a stop we got off and got our luggage. That's when I saw James' cousin for the first time.

"There she goes," James said. "Ressie, Ressie! Here we are! Over here!" James shouted.

Hearing her name called, she spotted us, and hurried over to greet us. Ressie and James embraced, and told each other how good it was to see one another. Then James introduced us. "Louise, this is my cousin, La Resse Williams, (fictional name) but we call her Ressie for short." "Hi, I'm pleased to meet you. I heard so much about you," I said, smiling.

"Girl, if James told you about me, ain't no telling what he done said," she jokingly replied.

I noticed Ressie was a good-looking woman and the family resemblance was obvious.

"Y'all come on. The van is out front," she said.

So we loaded up the van with our belongings and we drove back to her house.

While on the way to Ressie's, I gazed out the window and I could see that Racine was a beautiful town. It looked so promising. It seemed to be about the same size as Vicksburg, maybe a tad larger. What I noticed right away was that it was cooler up here, but that was all right because I could do without all the heat.

After we parked in front of Ressie's house, I got out of the car and began to help James unload our luggage, and that's when I could hear loud music blaring from her house. There were people laughing out loud as if though there was a party going on in there. Apparently, there was a card game on because you could hear the sound of cards, as they were being slapped down on a card table. The musty smell of cigarette smoke filled the air. Ressie's guests that were playing cards were also drinking liquor and beer. Being shocked, my countenance suddenly changed, and with dismay, I looked at James as if to say to him, *What in the world have you gotten us into?* Then Ressie walked right on back to the dining room where her guests were playing cards. She sat right down and began playing, as if though she'd never missed a hand.

Once we got there Ressie, seemed to have forgotten that we were out-of-town guests. By this time we were tired and hungry, but Ressie was still preoccupied with her company and her card game. She was quite indifferent. She didn't fix us any food or show us the least bit of decent hospitality. I couldn't believe it.

I then remembered her saying, "If you're hungry, there's some lunch meat in the refrigerator. Just go right ahead and help yourself."

After riding on that bus for eighteen hours, traveling over a thousand miles, we were offered cold sandwiches to satisfy our hunger. Right then and there, I knew these living arrangements were not going to work out. There was no way I was going to allow my family to live in a house where the hostess lacked hospitality and a bunch of mess was going on. It's not that I thought we were better than them. But the lifestyle they were living, is exactly what we were leaving behind in Kinson. Besides, there were too many of us to live comfortably at Ressie's house, so I began to seek the Lord on where we would go from here.

Well, to get away from all the commotion going on at Ressie's house, I asked her if she knew the location of a good, sanctified church. Ressie didn't know anything about a church, but she told me one of her in-laws named Patricia (fictional name) might know where a church was. She told me that she would call her to see if she could recommend a church. Ressie did just as she said and made the phone call. After hanging up, Ressie informed me that Patricia knew where a good church was and she would be over soon to meet me. Now that was good news and already I began to see some light at the end of the tunnel.

Later on that evening Patricia came to Ressie's house to meet me. She was a very nice lady with a warm and friendly spirit. After talking for a short while, she took me to her church. Although I can't recall the name of that church, it was certainly spirit filled. It had been a while since I'd been to such an anointed service like that one. Though it was only twenty or so members there, we sho-nuff had church that night. During the testimony service, I testified about all that the Lord had done in our lives. I then made a request and asked the saints to pray that the Lord would provide us with suitable living arrangements. After the preacher had finished preaching, he called for the prayer line, and I was one of the first in line. When it came time for me to receive prayer the minister asked that the congregation agree with us in prayer. My prayer request was that the Lord would make a way for us to find a better place to live. Then he began to pray and lay hands on me and I began to feel the peace of God in my spirit and I knew that somehow some way, God was going to intervene on our behalf. Therefore, I went back to Ressie's home, believing God was going to make a way.

Early the next morning, James received a phone call from one of his other relatives named Paula (fictional name). Apparently, the word had gotten around that James was in town with his family and Ressie's house was not big enough for us to stay. Who knows? Maybe Ressie called her. I really don't know. At any rate, while James and I were looking for another house, the Lord had put it on Paula's heart to let us stay with her. Although Paula wasn't a Christian either, she didn't have all of that commotion going on that Ressie had back at her place. This was a blessing within itself. So in two days, God moved on our behalf and we only ended up spending one night at Ressie's house.

After moving over to Paula's, I prayed and asked the Lord's guidance in finding us a house. So the Lord put it in my spirit, to search the Yellow Pages for a real estate agent. Therefore, under the leading of the Lord, I began to search the phone book as prompted. Since there were so many real estate agents in the phone book to choose from, I prayed again and asked the Lord to show me a particular one.

As I ran my finger down the column of real estate agents, I suddenly stopped on one. "Call this one," the Spirit directed.

So I picked up the phone, and as I began to dial the number, I remembered the passage of Scripture, where the Lord told his disciples, if they had faith the size of a mustard seed, that they could speak to those mountains, and they shall be moved.[5] Although I had never seen, nor heard of this real estate agent up until that day, I believed that my mustard seed of faith was about to move a mountain.

After I dialed the number, the phone rang for a long time. Finally, a man answered the phone. I introduced myself and went on to tell him that I was a wife and a mother of seven children. I told him that we were from out of town and desperately needed a place to stay. I told him that we had no money, and both my husband and I were unemployed, but in faith, I asked him to give us thirty days and in that time we'd have jobs. Then the real estate agent replied, "Yes, as a matter of fact, I believe

I do have a house that needs some work done on it. It might be just right for you. Would you like to see it?" he asked.

"Yes, we would," I excitedly replied.

So after making all the necessary arrangements, I hung up the phone, and I began to praise the Lord. "Hallelujah! Thank you, Jesus!" I shouted aloud. I was happy and full of joy. Yes, as the old Gospel song says, "Can't nobody do me like Jesus."

Although we had no money or jobs, God blessed us with a beautiful place to stay. After all the apartments that we lived in over the years, this was our first house. Yes, it was going to be my house. I was so excited about the opportunity the Lord had given us.

Since we only had a few possessions, moving to our new house was relatively easy. After we arrived and saw the house for the first time, it was apparent that there was quite a bit of work to be done. The exterior paint was cracking and peeling, and the grass hadn't been cut in a long time. On the inside, the house was even worse. The floor needed some repair, the ceiling was dropping in several places, and there were holes in the walls that needed patching. Boy oh boy, you name it, it needed fixing. After James and I took a tour of the house, we both knew that the task wouldn't be easy. However, even though the house required much cosmetic repair, the utilities were functioning, and it was structurally sound.

Another problem we had to address was the fact that we didn't have a single piece of furniture. For the first few days we practically did everything on the floor, so I called Patricia and told her what we needed. She in return made it known among her congregation that the Hunters needed help. Soon the members of her church responded in a bountiful way. It was absolutely amazing. Lamps, chairs, beds, tables, and clothes were some of the many items donated by the members of the church. Soon, our once empty house had furniture in practically every room. It was truly amazing to see the Lord respond to our situation in our time of need.

Four days after we had moved into our home, I went out looking for a job. Once again the Lord gave me favor. A well-to-do couple named Mr. and Mrs. Johnson, who owned a large beautiful home, offered me a job keeping house. With all the kids that we had, I was an expert at keeping house, so I saw this as an opportunity and eagerly accepted the job. When I came home and told James the good news, he didn't seem to be very happy. I could tell that he was disgusted about still being unemployed. Besides, we had to fulfill our end of the renovation agreement we made with our landlord, so while I went to work, James stayed home caring for the children and repairing the house.

Soon after I had started my new job, Mrs. Johnson, and I were talking and I told her about the predicament that our family was in. I told her about James being unemployed and how it was a struggle to have recently moved from Vicksburg. I guess she really felt sorry for me because I was working while I was seven months pregnant. That's when Mrs. Johnson told me that they owned a junk yard, and she would speak to Mr. Johnson concerning James.

Once again we found favor because Mr. Johnson hired James the next day. However, when I went back to work, Mrs. Johnson told me that I really shouldn't be working so hard while I was pregnant. She paid me and said, "A woman's place is in the home."

This was actually a welcomed change because it was hard working at this stage of pregnancy. Since James was now gainfully employed, we could now afford the rent and stay in our house beyond the original thirty-day agreement. It really did James a lot of good to be working a steady job once again. Mr. Johnson and James seemed to get along well, so he continued to work at the junk yard for a few years.

As the years went by, I continued to go to church and serve God and my faith increased a great deal. It seemed as if though whenever I called on the name of Jesus, the Lord would move on my behalf. Early in the mornings, I would rise up out of bed, having a spirit of thanksgiving and praise. Yes, the mornings were always a special time that I set aside to commune with the Lord. Like a daily ritual, I would get up early in the morning and take a hot relaxing bath so I could meditate.

While in peaceful meditation, I would often hear the Lord speak to my heart. When situations would arise where there was a lot of confusion, it was difficult to make good decisions. Oh, but let me get a good night's rest and get in that tub the next morning. Then my mind would be clear enough to hear from God. Yes, the Lord was teaching me never to make hasty decisions but how to wait on him. Little did I know at the time the Lord had something great in store for me.

As the years passed us by, I continued to have more and more children. If I were to count the two children that I miscarried, it would be a total of twenty-one children. I can remember delivering twelve children right in Racine. My name had become like a household name in the maternity ward because of my many pregnancies. Every time I would have a baby I would always ask the doctor to let me go home the next day. The doctor would always say, "No, Louise. You need to be in bed resting."

Then I would always tell the doctor, "Doctor, I can not leave my other babies at home by themselves. I have to be there for my little children."

"Well, all right, Louise, if you say so, but if you experience any complications, call us right away," the doctor would insist.

So I would leave the hospital not yet fully recovered and head home to care for my family. I just couldn't bear the thought of leaving my other children at home. I always felt very strongly about my children. Just as a mother hen gathers and cares for her little chicks, so would I protect and love all my children.

In the meantime, while I was having all these babies, James' bad habits once again crept back into our lives. After working years for Mr. Johnson at the junk yard, James got hired by the Case Company, a division of International Harvester. By this time we had to move to another house because our family kept on increasing. Since James was making good money at Case, we could afford a bigger place. The only problem was when the money increased, James' support, began to decrease. The only thing that James ever wanted to do was drink and stay out all night. Soon James got to the point where he wouldn't even come home at all. He just couldn't control his desire for cheap whiskey and no good women.

James was notorious for not coming home on payday weekends. It got to the place where the kids and I would go for days without enough food because James would be out, gallivanting and carousing around Racine. Well, enough was enough. One payday I gathered up our children and walked down to the Case Plant. My intentions were to catch James and get some money before he would go out and blow it. On a few occasions, I was fortunate enough to do just that, but it wasn't long before James got wise to us waiting for him.

One sunny Friday afternoon the kids and I went down to the Case Plant. It was payday and I wanted to catch James before he went out and spent all of his money. We arrived at the employee entrance right before the shift had ended, so all thirteen of my children and I found a place to sit down near the employee's entrance. I am sure we were a curious sight to see, but at this point, I didn't care how it looked; I needed to catch James before it was too late. As soon as the whistle sounded, and the employees began to come out, we waited and waited for James. A half hour went by. An hour went by and James still had not come out of the plant yet.

Frustrated and tired of waiting, I went up to the security guard and said, "I'm here to meet my husband, Mr. James Hunter, but he hasn't come out of the plant yet. Could you check to see if he had to work late or something?"

So after the guard called around to all the other gates, he informed me that James had left out of the back gate, over a half hour ago.

Once again James had found a way to evade us, this time by slipping out of the back gate. So there I stood, embarrassed and broke. I had nothing but bad news to give to my hungry little children.

"Mama, where's Daddy at?" they asked me, again and again. "Mama, I'm hungry. When are we gonna eat?" they wondered.

I felt terrible. How do you explain to a hungry little child that their father won't be providing for them? It took everything I had to hold back my tears that day. And while fighting back the tears my anger fueled my determination to survive.

James' infidelity and irresponsibility took its toll on us all, especially the children. Since he was gone so much, the kids began to suffer for it. By this time I had thirteen growing children that needed their father. When James was behaving well, he would spend quality time with the kids. However, he would often make them promises he simply wouldn't keep. Especially on special occasions, James would break his promises and often let us down. Since children are innocent and don't know any better, they believe whatever their parents tell them, especially if they are promised gifts for birthdays and Christmas. Even though I did my best to make up for his inconsistency, year after year, my children sat at home with no gifts from their father.

I would minister to my children and tell them that life is hard and that people don't always do what they're supposed to do. It was times like these that I had to be both the mother and the father to my children. In the midst of these trying times, I turned this situation into an opportunity to witness to my children. I told them, their father was a good man, but sometimes even good people make bad choices. Then I told them that, Jesus nor I, would never leave or forsake them.

It wasn't long after those lean Christmases that the Lord showed his glory and faithfulness. One Christmas season, while unbeknownst to us, our names were turned in to a charitable organization that helped struggling families. As it turned out, people from the community brought us so many gifts that we hardly had room to receive them. There were dolls, wagons, trains, clothes, and candy, everything that you could name. It really did my heart a lot of good to see my babies happy on Christmas morning. I said to my kids, "See there? I told you that if we trust in the Lord, he would see us through."

I was truly thankful to the Lord for all He had done for us. It was one of the best and most memorable Christmases that I ever experienced. We all had plenty. So we gave thanks to the Lord for what he had done for us. We played, prayed, and sang Christmas songs together all day long. God really shed his grace upon us abundantly.

As God continued to bless us, things were slowly improving for our family. James had slowed down his nightlife activities and was staying home more. Therefore, we were able to work on mending things back together again. We were even blessed with another house, located on Racine Street. It was a nice four-bedroom house a little larger than where we previously lived, but it was still too small for my thirteen, soon to be fourteen children. Yet we moved in any way and had been living there for a few weeks.

Up here in Wisconsin, the winters were so long and cold. This particular winter was a really bad one, and there were tons of snow. Old man winter had really tightened his arctic grip and temperatures plummeted below zero. One cold and blustery day there was a loud startling knock at the door. I thought, *Who in the world can this be, knocking loud like that.* "Who is it?" I asked.

"Sheriff's department. Is this the Hunter residence?" he asked.

The sheriff's department? Why would the sheriff be coming to my house? In a split second all kinds of thoughts raced through my mind. The first thing I thought of was something must have happened to James, so I opened the door and asked him if I could help him. Once again he asked me, "Is this the Hunter residence?"

I responded, "Yes. I'm Louise Hunter. What may I help you with, officer?"

"Mrs. Hunter, a complaint has been filed against your family, with the Board of Health, down at City Hall. The complaint states that there are too many people living here in this house." Then he said, "How many children do you have, Mrs. Hunter?"

"Thirteen," I replied.

"Then there's you and your husband as well. Fifteen total ma'am?"

"That's correct," I replied.

"I'm sorry, ma'am, I'm going to have to serve you with this eviction notice. Too many people living in this house presents health and safety issues. You have thirty days to vacate these premises," he ordered.

"But, officer, we have nowhere to go. If you put us out on the street, we'll be homeless. Where will I go with so many children?" I desperately asked.

He then responded by saying, "I'm sorry, ma'am. I don't know what to tell you. You understand. I'm just doing my job."

After saying that, he handed me the eviction notice. I was absolutely stunned. As I began to look it over, I was so perplexed that I could barely speak. As despair began to overwhelm me, tears dropped from my eyes. My reaction to this awful news was clear and I'm sure it touched the sheriff's heart. It must have been terrible to be the bearer of bad news, but there wasn't anything that he could do about it. Like he said, he was just doing his job. As he turned and walked out of the house, I slowly shut the door behind him. I fell back against the door and began to ask, "My God, what are we going to do now?"

As I had experienced so many times in the past, once again, my back was against the wall and I didn't know what I was going to do. Why Jesus? Why Lord? When is my suffering going to end? Not long ago, Lord, you blessed us with this house. Now in the middle of winter, the sheriff has come to cast us out onto the streets of Racine. When James came home that evening, I told him what had happened. Initially, he was worried, but he tried to be as positive as he could. I really appreciated James' optimism, but in this situation, we were going to need more than just positive thinking. We needed nothing short of a miracle.

Well, just as I had done before, I went to the Yellow Pages to find a real estate agent and I even called the one that helped us out before, but this time none of the real estate agents were able to help us. We also called friends and neighbors. We searched magazines and newspapers. No matter where we looked, or to whom we turned, there was no help to be found.

As the eviction date drew closer, the tension began to mount, but I continually labored before the Lord in prayer and supplication. I sought the Lord as I have never sought him before, asking him to intervene once more on our behalf, but still nothing came through for us. I needed an answer from the Lord, but He was silent. I thought, *My God, what do you do when you need an answer from the Lord and He is silent?*

Now that the thirty-day deadline had been imposed, the days seemed to go by so fast. The day before the eviction date, our backs were up against the wall with no hope of finding a new residence in sight. The night before the sheriff was to come, both James, and I were very restless fearing what we thought would be inevitable, but as the hours ticked by, we managed to fall asleep amidst all our anxiety. The next thing I knew, my alarm clock awakened me. It was now 4:30 a.m.

I got up out of bed and I began to cry out to the Lord. *Lord Jesus, I need a miracle for my family. Lord, we have nowhere to go and no one else can help us but You.*

Yes, indeed I poured myself out to the Lord in prayer and supplication. Trusting in what the Bible tells us that, the Lord is a present help in the time of trouble.[6] After I finished praying, I got dressed and prepared myself for the day. After praying, my spirit was at peace. I was confident that the Lord was going to move on our behalf. As morning slipped away, it was now approaching the noon hour.

Since I hadn't heard from the sheriff's department yet, I started thinking maybe they wouldn't be around today after all. Maybe God has somehow delayed their coming for us. I was trying my best to see some light in this situation, but as the hands on the clock struck noon, there came the old familiar knock at the door, both loud and authoritative. My heart shuddered and I began to breathe deeply.

*This is it*, I thought, as I slowly made my way to the door. I didn't have to ask who it was because deep down inside I knew who it was. I tried my best to collect my thoughts, so I took a deep breath and nervously asked, "Who is it?"

"Racine County Sheriff's Department. Could you open the door please?"

When I opened the door the cold air of that blustery winter day rushed into the house. There stood the same deputy sheriff that had served the eviction notice thirty days earlier. "Step in," I said.

He came in and closed the door behind him.

"I'm sorry, ma'am. Your thirty days have expired and we have come to enforce the eviction."

This was one of the most desperate moments of my life, the circumstances were dismal, there was nothing that I could say or do. By this time my children had begun to wander up to the door. One by one, they wanted to see to who their mama was talking with.

As my children came to the door, something interesting began to happen. The expression on the officer's face began to change. I guess he had never seen so many kids in one house before. His eyes had now begun to divert from me to my children. Occasionally he'd look down at my protruding stomach as I was nine months' pregnant at the time. And that's when the Spirit of the Lord prompted me to say. "If you could please find it in your heart to give us just a few more days to find a home, I would greatly appreciate it. Please, officer, we haven't found anywhere to go yet."

With that he shrugged his shoulders and said, "Ma'am, I can't. I've got to do my job," but even as he spoke, the Lord began to move on his heart. His eyes kept on looking at all my children and my swollen belly. As sympathy began to overtake him, he took a deep breath, looked me in the eyes and said, "OK, Mrs. Hunter."

He turned and opened the door and stepped out of the house. As he began to walk down the porch stairs, he turned back and said, "I'll be back in a few days."

He got into his car, shut the door and slowly pulled away down the snow-covered street. After closing the door behind me, I felt a great surge of relief. The Lord had lifted this great weight off my shoulders. How great is the power of our God. Jesus moved on this man's heart allowing time for God to work an even greater miracle, on the following day.

When James finally came home later that night, I told him all about what had happened. I was so excited about what God had done, but James didn't seem to understand. He couldn't see God's hand at work in this situation. Unlike James, I believed that Jesus was going to work this out, so I began to praise God as never before. With all of my being, I offered up the sacrifice of praise. I'm sure James must have thought I was crazy, but at that point, I didn't care. My heart was fixed and my mind was stayed on Jesus and I trusted in what the Scriptures declare that, "…If God be for us, who can be against us."[7] When I went to sleep that night, I was at peace and in full assurance that God was going to make a way out of no way.

The next morning came and I woke up with the joy of the Lord in my heart. I was anxious to see what God was going to do for us. Deep in my heart I knew things were going to be all right. I didn't know how, nor where our blessing was going to come, but I knew God was going to intervene on our behalf.

Well, I hadn't been up long, maybe about and hour or two, it was still early in the morning. All of a sudden there was a knock at the door but it wasn't like the loud intrusive knock of the deputy sheriff. No, it was different all together. There was a peace about it that evoked no fear. So I hurried to the door. "Who is it?" I asked.

"Excuse me, ma'am, sorry to bother you so early in the morning, but my name is Reverend Nicholson. May I have a word with you please?"

*Nicholson*, I mused. *I don't know any preachers named Nicholson.* I opened the door, and there stood Reverend *Nicholson*. He was wearing a brown over coat and a dark brown hat.

He gave me a warm smile and said, "I'm sorry to bother you, but I just need a few minutes of your time."

"Sure, come on in," I replied.

So he stepped in and closed the door behind him. "What can I help you with, Reverend?" I asked.

Then he said, "No, I came to help you. I know we've never seen each other before, but I think I might have something you might need."

"What is it?" I asked.

Then he said, "I have a house for you."

He went on to say that a woman he knew had a house and wanted to give it to somebody and our family's name was mentioned to her.

As he was telling me about the house, I was completely amazed. The spirit of excitement began to dispel the fear and gloom that had taken us captive. I could finally begin to see the light of hope peering through the dark shadows of despair. So I asked him, "Where's this house located?"

"610 North Randolph Street," he replied. "Would you like to see it?"

"Yes, of course. Let me ask my husband if I can go with you to see it!" I excitedly replied, so I hurried back to our bedroom, to ask James if I could go and see this house.

"James, James, honey, wake up. Listen, there's a man named Rev. Nicholson here, and he's come to show us a house. I need to go with him to take a look at it. You don't mind if I go with him do you?"

"What! You're kidding, ain't cha?" James asked.

"No, baby, I'm serious. He's out there in the living room right now, waiting to take me to go see the house."

After James saw how anxious I was, he got up out of bed, saying, "Wait a minute. Let me see who this is you're talking about."

So he put on his robe and came out into the living room.

"You know about some house or something, mister?" James asked. "Yes, sir, I was just telling the misses about it."

"Baby, can I go with him?" I anxiously interrupted.

"Yes, go, but you be careful out there, Louise," he replied.

James was concerned about me moving roundabout so much because I was expecting our fourteenth child any day now. So I put on my coat, and Reverend Nicholson got the door and helped me down the stairs and out to his car. Then off we went to go see this miracle house. We drove to Randolph Street, which was only a few blocks away from our house on Racine Street. When we pulled up in front of the house I could see it was a beautiful home. It was a rather large two-story white frame house.

"Here we are, Mrs. Hunter," he said. After we'd both gotten out of the car, he helped me up the stairs. When he opened the front door, he smiled and said, "After you, Mrs. Hunter."

With amazement, I anxiously entered this beautiful house. As we walked through the house I saw all the lovely rooms. I just kept thinking, it's perfect and enough space to accommodate our large family. Then I said, "Reverend Nicholson, a house so large must cost a fortune to rent, we have no money. My husband works at Case, but he only makes one hundred and forty dollars a week and we have no savings. We couldn't possibly afford to rent a house this size."

"The woman who is offering the house doesn't want to rent it out. This house is only for sale. And you have to take it today," he insisted.

"For sale," I replied.

"I'm afraid so, Mrs. Hunter. The lady wants to sell it to a family who'll appreciate it and take care of it."

When he said that, it was if though all hope had been snatched away from us. I began the think about our credit being too bad to be approved for a mortgage, and then there's the closing cost, taxes and all the other expenses of buying a home. I just knew this was beyond our reach. However, in the midst of these overwhelming odds, I nervously asked, "How much does she want for it?"

Reverend Nicholson paused, took a deep breath and then he smiled and to my surprise replied, "One dollar."

"What! One dollar!" I exclaimed.

"That's right, Mrs. Hunter. This house is yours for just one dollar." I couldn't believe my ears. So I anxiously searched through my purse and then all my pockets, but, wouldn't you know it, a chance of a lifetime and I didn't have a single dollar to my name. So I told him, "I'm sorry, Rev. Nicholson, but I don't even have the dollar on me but if you'll drive me back home I'm sure my husband has a dollar." Reverend Nicholson chuckled slightly, smiled and said, "That's okay, Mrs. Hunter. I'll pay the dollar for you."

"Oh thank you, Reverend Nicholson. God bless you. Thank you so much, God has truly sent you to be a blessing to my family and I'll never forget it," I joyfully replied.

And with that, the tears of joy began to flow. I had never been so tremendously blessed in all of my life. From the depths of my heart, I began to thank and praise the Lord, and then I began to shout,

"Hallelujah." I was practically hysterical with joy. It was as if nothing else in the world mattered, I was going to give God the glory. It was no time to be dignified. I offered up the sacrifice of praise to Lord with all of my might.

Once again the Lord was faithful and delivered the Hunter family. Jesus saved us from the uncertainty of homelessness. He delivered us from being cast out onto the cold wintry streets of Racine, Wisconsin. Just when hope was lacking and the darkness seemed to prevail, the Son of God shined the light of hope in our lives. With His great loving arms, He reached out, touched us, and saved us from the pits of disparity. He walked right into our situation and He made it work out together for the good. This is what the Lord can do for you when you put your trust in Him.

Jesus said in His Word that He would never leave or forsake you. And I also remembered what it says in the Psalms: "I have been young, and now am old; yet have I not seen the righteous forsaken, nor His seed begging bread. He is ever merciful, and lendeth; and His seed is blessed."[8] Surely God was teaching me that in the midst of trials and tribulations we should stand on the promises of God.

Yes, I praised the Lord with all of my heart, mind, and soul. I gave it all to Jesus that day. And my heart was fixed. Lord I want to serve you! Lord I want to live for you! Jesus Christ my Lord and Savior, what will you have me to do? Oh Lord, you have done the greatest thing for me. What is it Lord that you will have me to do for you? I asked over and over. Humbling myself before the Lord, I made myself available for Jesus. Just like the Bible says, be a living sacrifice holy and acceptable to God, for reasonable service.[9]

After what God did for me, serving Him for the rest of my life was certainly the reasonable thing to do. And that's when I made up my mind, that I would spend my life helping others that have nowhere to go and no one to love them. Relating to my own experiences, I knew what it was like to be hungry. I knew what it was like to have hungry little children. I knew what it was like to be a stranger, and have no one to turn to. I knew what it was like to be rejected and downtrodden. And I also knew what it was like to have Jesus come into my life and deliver me when all else failed. He gave me sight when I was blind. He gave me hope when times were hard, and I had no one else to turn to.

Therefore, in my prayer I said, *Lord, there are so many of your people that are hurting, lonely and broken-hearted, just like I was. Jesus, all I want to do with my life is help some of these people. If you let me, Lord, I will help them, and tell them all about your amazing grace.*

I really poured myself out before the Lord that day. After experiencing his mercy so many times, I felt obligated to tell others about His love, mercy and grace. I then began to feel a great sense of purpose, as if the Lord had been leading me down a predestinated path all the time. Suddenly I began to realize my suffering had not been in vain, but was part of God's master plan for my life. I had been tried, tested and now it was time to do a great work for the Lord.

# Chapter 5
## Manifest Destiny

Two months had now come and gone since we had moved into our new home. I still hadn't gotten over the magnificent, miraculous manner in which the Lord intervened on our behalf. It was as if the joy and excitement over our new house were being renewed each day. Whenever I looked out my window onto the cold streets, I was reminded of where we could have been. Therefore, I was thankful and would praise God and continually seek his direction on what he would have me to do in His service. I wanted so badly to serve the Lord. I was willing to do anything He asked of me. I was willing to make any sacrifice to show my gratitude for His graciousness.

Early one morning, about 2 a.m., I suddenly woke up out of my sleep. All was quiet in the house. However, something was troubling my spirit. I couldn't get back to sleep. My husband and my children were all sound asleep. Then suddenly, while lying in my bed, I looked up at the ceiling, and as I was doing so, a mysterious state of spiritual ecstasy came over me. As I lay motionless in the still of the night, I saw a vision. It was like the ceiling had opened up and I was looking into the heavens. In this great vision, I saw hundreds of children that appeared to be neglected. Their clothes were dirty, their hair was uncombed, and they were wandering with no one to care for them. Though they cried out for someone to help them, no one responded to their cries. They were in a helpless condition because they had no one to meet their needs. Aimlessly they wandered, desperate, despondent, and afraid. Being totally captivated yet saddened by this vision, their plight spoke directly to my heart. It was terrible. I could feel their rejection and pain. All I wanted to do was to love and comfort them. I wanted to aid and assist them, but just like being in a dream, I called out to them but they couldn't hear me. Aimlessly they wandered back and forth without hope or direction.

Then right before my eyes, the children turned older and older. It was like they spent their whole life wandering, now they were old men and women crippled and weak. There were great disparity and loneliness written all over their faces. They had no companionship and no one to comfort them. Then I heard the voice of the Lord say to me, "Gather the children together, and teach them my ways." Then the Lord spoke again and said: "Go to the aged and comfort them for they too are my children."

As I was beholding this great vision, the Lord's presence was heavy in the room. I could feel His anointing flowing through me, like a mighty river. I was becoming one with this glorious revelation like I was being impregnated with the desire to comfort those who are in need. The ministry of benevolence was now growing inside my innermost being. Like a woman pregnant with child, soon I would give birth to the ministry to which God had called me.

As I lay there in my bed, the Lord began to shed forth his love into my heart. Then He gave me the compassion for the young and the old. He also gave me the will to comfort those who were rejected and in distress. After this, the Lord began to take me back over the years of my life and he showed me that it was His hand that guided me through every situation. He had always been there. He never left me nor forsook me, but walked with me every painful step of the way. When I was a little girl, it was Jesus that moved on my mother's heart to open up the chest that my sister had locked me in. Otherwise, I would have died years ago back on the farm. It was Jesus that walked along with us through the hills and hollows of Warren County, protecting us as we walked miles to go to school each day. It was Jesus that comforted our hearts, those many nights we were afraid to sleep, after that horrible plane crash. It was Jesus that sent the woman from the health department, to tell me to repent of my sins, back in Vicksburg. It was Jesus that sent the strange woman, to warn me of the danger that was to come when Zoline was burned back in Kinson. It was Jesus that moved on the woman's heart at the real estate office in Kinson, who brought us food and paid our fare back to Vicksburg. It was Jesus that stayed the hand of the Racine County Sheriff's Department. It was Jesus that saved us from eviction by miraculously sending Reverend Hunter to bless us with our house.

As I recalled all these past events and circumstances, I could see the mighty hand of God, working out his plan for my life. Now it was becoming clear, there was a reason and a purpose for all the pain and rejection I suffered for so many years. Jesus was preparing me to serve Him. I was being tested and qualified in order to carry out a great commission. I was about to embark on a great and fulfilling work. Now my life had meaning. Now there was a greater purpose for me beyond being a wife and a mother.

A few days after I had this vision I wanted to tell my husband, but I didn't know how to explain it to him. However, I felt he should be the first to know. I thought to myself, surely God has already prepared his heart to receive this, but to my surprise, James didn't seem interested at all. I couldn't understand it. I was really disappointed, I just knew that God would have prepared my husband's heart for this great calling. No matter how hard I tried to explain the vision to James, he just wasn't getting it. Each time I brought it up, it only lead to an argument. After I realized that James wasn't buying into it, it only strengthened my resolve. I was determined, with or without him, to do the work that God had now called me to do.

Although I had no prior experience in the ministry and even though I had little education, I believed that God would give me the wisdom to start a benevolent work. Like anyone else, I wanted to know the end from the beginning. However, I learned that when the Lord calls us to do a specific work; we don't know all the details up front. We only know what He reveals as we go. It's like looking through a dark glass. Though we are beholding, what we see often lacks clarity. There are always many unanswered questions, and many blanks left to be filled in. However, one of the main ingredients that the Lord is looking for is faith and a willing heart. Though we may not have all the information in advance, we learn to trust in God as we walk in His will for our lives. As the Bible says, "…we walk by faith and not by sight."[10]

According to the vision, the first phase of the ministry was to teach the children about Jesus. This called for skills that I didn't know that I had until I trusted God and stepped out on faith. After spending time contemplating my next step, I decided to start up a Bible study for the neighborhood children. Once that issue was settled, I had to figure out a way to draw the children. Like the Scriptures said, "…he that wins souls is wise."[11] How can I do this Lord, I asked? As I pondered on this, I began to consider that the Lord often met the physical needs of the people first. So I realized that I must also use practical methods to draw the children to whom I was to minister. Here's where my maternal experience began to pay off.

I knew all children love sweets. Therefore, I put my mothering and baking skills to work. Years ago, back in Warren County, Mama used to make us little, "sweet cakes," as we called them back then. So from that same old family recipe, I learned back on the farm, I made sweet cakes for the children attending the Bible study. The Bible studies would start promptly at five p.m. This allowed enough time for the kids to come by after getting home from school.

I also realized that if I'm going to minister to the other children, my own kids should also participate. I knew that the neighborhood children would like to see kids in their own age group being involved in our program. Since music can be a universal language, I wanted to communicate in a language that the kids would understand and enjoy. Therefore, I encouraged my own children to form a singing group. We called ourselves the Hunter Singers. My boys and girls were all very talented. All of them could sing and play the different instruments as well. We would all spend hours rehearsing our praise songs, and sometimes, even James would play the drums for us. Yes, the Hunter singers were a dynamic family choir.

It all seemed so natural for them. They really put their hearts into it. I taught them how to sing to God's glory, just like my mother taught us back on the farm.

Each day before my kids left to go to school, I would always tell them, "Y'all bring some of your friends by after school now, and tell them about the Bible study, the singing group and the sweet cakes."

Well, it didn't take long for the word to spread among the kids that Mrs. Hunter was giving out tasty pastries after school. Pretty soon several children were coming to study the Bible, and to eat my delicious sweet cakes.

Before I'd begin the Bible study, we'd start out with prayer, and then we would sing praise songs. It made me so happy to see those kids singing those songs of praise. They really enjoyed singing along with our family choir. Besides, the singing made the Bible study fun for them. As we all know, children have such short attention spans so I made it enjoyable, because no one likes a boring worship service.

# Love and Charity

Dynamic Family Choir
Photo by William Lizdas, *Journal Times*, Racine, Wis., 12/8/74

While the Bible study would be going on, the aroma of the sweet cakes baking in the oven filled the house. All the kids anxiously anticipated sinking their teeth into those delectable little treats. After teaching for a while, I would have a little question and answer session. Whoever got the most questions right, I would give them an extra sweet cake.

Yes, the kids really enjoyed learning about the Lord and they always brought hefty appetites for both the word and my sweet cakes. One occasion I had started mixing up some sweet cakes and I ran out of sugar, so I substituted Karo syrup instead. As it turned out, this batch of cakes was the best batch that I had ever made. Ironically, several children received the Lord that day. Now I'm quite aware that it's the Holy Spirit which draws us to Calvary's cross. But on this day the Lord also used my sweet cakes, from an old family recipe, to gather the little children unto him. Yes, indeed the Bible does, in fact, declare, "O taste and see that the LORD is good...."[12]

Right away you could notice the difference in the neighborhood because the children were no longer hanging out on the street corners and getting into mischief. After a while, there were as many as thirty-five children in my Bible studies. My neighbors really appreciated the fact that someone was concerned enough about the children's welfare to take action. While conducting the Bible studies, I began to see these children had other needs as well. My heart would really go out to them all. So often they were very withdrawn, and some harder to reach than others, but they all responded well to love.

The more heartbreaking cases were the children whose parents were alcoholics or on drugs. These kids were the hardest to reach. Due to the surroundings, they were raised in, it was hard for them to trust or receive love from others. Since they lacked love and were attention starved, they could be very restless and would act out the most. But through the love they received from us, the emotional barriers they erected would eventually come down.

For many kids, they never learned day-to-day things, such as physical hygiene and good table manners. Since their parents didn't teach them, they didn't know any better, so we had to be patient with them and show them the right way to do things. But in spite of it all, the love that we gave them prevailed and was the single most important factor that helped to change their lives.

In the Bible, it says, "For God so loved the world, that He gave His only begotten Son…."[13] The part of this Scripture that impacted me the most was, God *so loved*…that *He gave*. The most important thing to realize is, love is an action word. Love will cause you to give to people, no matter who they are, or what condition that they're in. No matter what we do, if it's not done in love, it really means nothing. This is why the Bible tells us, there are three dynamics to a fulfilling spiritual life, which are, faith, hope, and love. However, of these three, love or charity is the greatest of them all.

With that in mind, I wanted to give the ministry a name that adequately portrays what it was that we endeavored to do. It was my heartfelt purpose to meet the needs of hurting people. I didn't just want to be a charity so to speak. I wanted people to experience God's love just as we had. Since God had demonstrated His amazing love to me time after time and I saw how effective love was in changing people's lives. I named the ministry, the Love and Charity Club Inc.

For four years, right from my own home at 610 Randolph Street, the Love and Charity Club ministered to the needs of the children and teens of Racine. With the success we experienced over the years with the youth, I was determined to do more for Jesus in the community. I was ready to move on to other aspects of ministry, but my home wasn't large enough, to accommodate the increasing number of people needing assistance, so I sought the Lord for a building to base our operation out of, and soon my prayers were answered.

One day a friend brought me word of a storefront space for rent on State Street. It was in a good location, not too far from the downtown area. I contacted the owner and made arrangements to rent the property. Although the monthly rental fee was reasonable, I really didn't know where the money would come from to pay rent and utilities. However, once again I stepped out on faith and began to rally support from my neighbors. Since the Love and Charity Club had been a blessing to the community for so long, the people gladly helped us. My neighbors anxiously donated just about everything that we needed, everything from food to furniture. In no time at all, the Love and Charity Club was up and running. I was so thrilled at how the Lord was bringing everything together so quickly. To add the finishing touch, I had a beautiful sign painted up to hang outside the club. In big colorful letters, the sign says, *Louise Hunter Love and Charity Club*.

Our Grand Opening
(Louise and James Hunter, with Mrs. Moses Gracia)
Photo by Chuck D'Acquisto, *Journal Times*, Racine, Wis., 7/1/70

On the morning of July 1st, 1970, we officially opened up in our new location at 1210 State Street. I called Racine's own, *Journal Times* newspaper to see if they would come to cover our opening. I wasn't sure whether they would actually see our opening as being newsworthy. However, to my surprise, *Journal Times* staff reporter, Barbara Heffling came out that morning along with the photographer Chuck D'Acquisto and got the complete scoop on the new Love and Charity Club. I was so elated about making the newspapers. This was the first time that I had ever been in the papers. It was exhilarating because all this notability was something very new to me. However, I wasn't alone. My husband James Hunter, our first vice president, and Mrs. Moses Garcia, our first secretary and treasurer, stood with me in front of our new storefront location.

After the *Journal Times* did the story, the news about Love and

Charity, became the talk of the town. In the wake of all this new publicity with the Love and Charity Club, I remembered the second phase of the vision was to comfort the elderly. So I asked my neighbors and friends if they knew of any elderly people that needed any help. After making those inquiries, I had a long list of senior citizens who were in need of our services. So I could be better acquainted with the plight of the senior citizens that we were servicing, I started going along on the home visitations on a regular basis.

While doing my visitations, I soon discovered that these senior citizens were suffering from loneliness and boredom. It was so sad to see these once productive and hard-working citizens, dejected and forgotten. In many cases, their own children who they raised and provided for didn't have the compassion or decency to care for their own aging parents.

Another dilemma for the elderly was after being retired and living on fixed incomes, they didn't have enough money to make ends meet. If they received some form of state assistance or Social Security, it wasn't enough. On top of all these factors most of them suffered from some type of illness, and between visits to doctors and medications, their funds were further depleted. By the end of each month, they had no money for food nor basic necessities. This often meant they would have to go days on end without proper nourishment. Each time I would hear of these conditions, my heart would break.

When I tried to act as a liaison between them and social service agencies, I was disheartened when I discovered the lack of available resources for the elderly. Determined to make a difference in their lives, I started a food drive and began to collect canned goods to distribute to the senior citizens. I called this ministry, the Widow's Closet. I went around to neighbors, churches, and stores, to see if they would like to donate food for our community's senior citizens. Although there were a few people that didn't give, overall the response was great. Soon I had plenty of canned goods to distribute to meet the needs of Racine's aged needy.

Soon food for Widow's Closet distribution was piling up at our headquarters. However, many had no way of coming to get the food. So I called on friends and associates to set up a delivery network to get the food to those in need. Occasionally, when James came home from work, he had to fill in when others couldn't do the deliveries or pickups. Often, items like furniture and appliances needed repair before they could be distributed. Therefore, James had to be the handyman and do the repairs. However, the harder we worked and the more we gave to God's people, the more the Lord blessed us with what we needed for the ministry.

As the numbers of people who were blessed through the Widow's Closet began to increase, more people started volunteering their time and resources. Soon we had seventeen volunteers helping with the pickups, the donation distribution, and the Bible studies. We also maintained a twenty-four-hour hotline manned by my children and volunteers, to respond to any emergency referrals.

Although we operated on a shoestring budget, we had faith that the Lord would provide. However, there were months where we simply didn't have the donations to cover the rent. On more than one occasion, James paid the rent out of his paycheck. That meant on several occasions our family had to make some painful sacrifices. By and by, though we sacrificed, the Lord was faithful and provided for my large family.

I really got a lot of joy out of helping the disadvantaged. On many home visits, we would see the joy and happiness on the faces of those who received help from us. Many of the people just needed someone to lend them an ear, so whenever we came around we would listen to what they had to say. We would always pray for them, and read to them

Bible passages, to comfort their lonely hearts. The fact that someone cared about them meant so much. Tears of joy would often flow from their eyes while we were spending quality time with them. Whereas in the past they were often treated as castaways, now God had raised up the Widow's Closet and the Love and Charity Club to be a companion and support. We were the ray of hope that brightened up the lives that had been overshadowed and darkened by loneliness.

The word about the Love and Charity Club and the Widow's Closet, started spreading to the neighboring townships like Kenosha, Franklin, and Sturtevant. Support started pouring in as we endeavored to help everyone we could. As I reached out to these surrounding townships, I began to see that there was a greater need than what I first realized. Homelessness, poverty, and disparity were no longer big city phenomena. Now small town USA was also experiencing the effects of the foul economic winds that were blowing throughout America.

Due to the increased numbers of those who had nowhere to get a decent meal, I opened up a food line. This, too, proved to be another big success for the Love and Charity Club. Once I started the food line, many of the Racine's food merchants got involved and donated lots of food. I would receive large bread and pastry donations from the neighborhood bakers, and soups, meats, and produce from restaurants and grocery stores. As the people lined up for the hot meals we prepared, I also gave out Gospel tracks. I never lost sight of the fact that this was the Lord's ministry, therefore, reaching people with the Gospel was the most important thing. After all, the whole purpose of the love that I was showing them was to point them to Jesus Christ. In keeping with the vision, I continued to have daily Gospel and prayer services, as a way to address our clients' spiritual needs.

We also did a lot of Christian counseling because we encountered so many people that were depressed and close to giving up on life. My heart particularly went out to those women who had been abandoned by their husbands. With all the heartbreak that I suffered because of James, I could personally relate to their situations when they would ask me how did I make it? This gave me the opportunity to share my testimony. When I would tell hurting women about the seemingly impossible situations that Jesus delivered me from, they realized that they weren't so bad off after all. Women would always marvel that I was able to make it, especially with all the children that I have. I would emphasize the fact that I stayed with Jesus even though I had been through some very tough times in my own marital life.

Speaking from my own experiences, I always told people no matter what the situation, don't give up. Cast your care upon Jesus because He will see you through. Yes, as it says in the Bible, we overcome the devil by the blood of the Lamb and the word of our testimony.[14]

As time moved on, I started being referred to as, Racine's "Mother Teresa." Though I was flattered by being compared with such a great humanitarian, I could not get sidetracked by all the accolades. It was important that I stayed focused on the vision that God gave me. I knew that there was still much more work to do in our city. Therefore, I had to guard against becoming complacent. Even though I gave myself whole heartily to the ministry, I quickly learned that balance and prioritizing was very important to maintain healthy relationships. After all, I was a wife, and the mother of sixteen children, each one of them needed their mother's love and attention.

# Chapter 6
## A Shelter Is Born

One sunny Monday morning, I made a startling discovery that changed the scope of Love and Charity forever. After opening up, I noticed some trash in one of our trash cans that needed emptying. Apparently one of our volunteers forgot to empty all the garbage cans. So when I opened the back door to go out to the dumpster, to my surprise, I found people sleeping in the alley out behind the Love and Charity Club. I couldn't believe it. So I asked them, "Y'all been out here all night waiting for me to open up?"

One man stood up and said, "Yes, ma'am. We have nowhere to go, Mrs. Hunter," he replied. "This is the only place in town we could come to get something to eat. So we have been waiting here all night."

When I heard this, my heart was filled with compassion for them. I felt that there must be something more that I could do. The Lord had provided my family with a place to lay our heads, but there were so many others that had nowhere safe to spend the night.

As much as I had been doing in the community I suddenly realized that it wasn't enough. There was still a great deal more that needed to be done. Fixing a few meals a day, and feeding the hungry was good, but it still wasn't enough. After they ate, they needed a safe place to lay their heads at night. I began to consider all the trouble people get themselves into, simply because they're out during the night. Being in the wrong place at the wrong time gets people into lots of trouble. The streets and alleys are no place for anybody to have to sleep.

Being impacted by this situation, I felt it was necessary to take another step of faith. Although there was little available room at my house, if a person really needed a place to sleep, I couldn't see turning them away. So I began to take the homeless into my own home. Initially, my hospitality was extended to the elderly or women with small children. To make them feel at home, we all shared with them like they were members of our own family.

Unfortunately, this was unsuitable for James. As far as he was concerned, being busy at the Love and Charity Club was already starting to strain our relationship, but once I started to take in strangers, James really started to protest. His whole attitude started changing for the worse, and his old ways started to show more and more. I knew what the problem behind James' bad behavior really was. Since the Lord was being glorified, the devil didn't like it. Therefore, one of the enemy's counter strategies was to try to discourage me through my husband's behavior. Now I had to stay on my knees before God and seek wisdom on how to balance both of these delicate issues. However, as much as I tried to be understanding and diplomatic, the tension kept building.

One day James and I had a terrible argument. James was complaining that he had enough and spoke about leaving.

And that's when I told him, "With or without you, I'm not going to stop serving Jesus, nor will I give up the work that the Lord has called me to do.

I'll die first before I let you or anybody else stand in the way of me and Love and Charity. If it means that you will walk out on me, then you go ahead. I'm staying with Jesus. If each of my children leaves home one by one and abandons me, I'm staying with Jesus. If it means that I'll have no friends, I don't care because there's a friend that sticks closer than a brother. His name is Jesus."

I knew all along that it cost you something to serve the Lord. It's a great responsibility, as well as a great sacrifice. God knows I loved my husband and all my children, but I would not compromise my commitment to the Lord's work. Though Satan fought me with everything in his arsenal, I remained steadfastly committed to the work that God called me to do.

As the fall of 1974 was coming to a close, the Thanksgiving season was upon us. It was a wonderful time because they were we able to feed a lot of people. I organized a turkey drive, and we were able to give away many turkeys that were donated to us from businesses and grocery stores alike. We also set up a food line and fed Racine's homeless as if they were dignitaries. We served turkey and dressing, ham and sweet potatoes, collard greens and ham hocks. For dessert, we served sweet potato pie, chocolate cake, and ice cream. You name it; we served it. To satisfy our spiritual appetites, some local churches sent their missionaries and ministers to conduct prayer and devotional services. Boy, oh Boy, we celebrated that Thanksgiving Day. We all gave praise to the Lord because we had so much to be thankful for. I reflected back on what God had done for me. I thanked Him for my health, all my children, and the ministry God gave me to oversee.

Soon the Christmas season was upon us, and it too was a big success. People from all over Racine County donated so many toys, clothes, and food that we hardly had enough room to hold them all. We were able to distribute all sorts of Christmas gifts to disadvantaged children that year. For those who could afford it, we asked for a small donation. Though the Love and Charity Club was a nonprofit organization, the financial gifts helped defray our operating expenses.

In all the years that Love and Charity have been operating, we never accepted state or government funds. It was primarily because I would have had to do away with all the religious services that we held. As far as I was concerned, prayer, praise, and worship services were even more important than the material things that we gave away. Jesus was the backbone of Love and Charity and there was no way I would compromise the religious services just to get funding from the government, so we were totally dependent on free-will offerings that the Lord put on people's hearts to give us. As for me, I never drew a salary, yet the Lord always provided for my family.

Though we usually had the finances to pay our utility bills on time, there came a time where we fell months behind. I can remember one year when our gas was cut off and winter came upon us. Though it was freezing outside, I kept the Love and Charity Club open, anyway. I couldn't bear the thought of someone who needed help showing up, and we'd be closed, so I stayed there with a few of my children. Although it was cold, we covered up in blankets to keep warm. I wasn't concerned so much about my own comfort, as I was for theirs, but my babies didn't seem to mind because they loved helping out at the club. From the very beginning, my children have been a part of Love and Charity.

As the afternoon drew on, James came to the club. This time, he really had hell in him.

"Woman, are you crazy? Got my kids sitting up here in the cold. What's wrong with you? Have you lost your cotton pick'n mind?" he shouted angrily.

"Ain't nobody asked you to be here, James. You can turn right back around and walk out that door. I will not close down Love and Charity because of the cold, for James Hunter, or for nothing else. I'm staying, James, until it's time to close," I replied.

"Woman, you need your head examined. Ain't nobody supposed to be that damned religious," he said furiously.

He then stormed out of the club, slamming the door behind him. After he left, you could hear a pin drop in the room. The kids and I, were too shocked to mutter a single word. I started thinking, *He ought to be ashamed of himself, showing out on me like that in front of the kids.* I was so angry at James that I almost started to cry, but as I have done on many occasions, I fought back the tears. I needed to be strong for my children. I didn't want them to see me broken because of this. My kids were terrified. It was quite unnerving for them to witness their father fly off the handle at me like that. So I sat back down and cuddled with my babies underneath the blanket. Then softly I said to them, "Don't ya'll worry. Everything's going to be all right. Daddy didn't mean it. He's not mad with you," I softly consoled.

As the temperature dropped further, time seemed to be at a standstill. Yet in the midst of the frigid room, we waited patiently for closing time to come. As it drew closer to five p.m., suddenly the door swung open. In stepped a man and a woman, shivering from the icy cold weather. I was so glad that we had stayed open because somebody really did need help.

"Mrs. Hunter, our heat is off back at our apartment. Do you have any extra blankets?" they kindly asked.

"Yes, we got a few left. You're welcome to them. Here, y'all take some canned goods and sandwiches home with you," I insisted.

"Thanks, Mrs. Hunter, we really appreciate it. God bless you," they aid as they went on their way. Although the only tangible things we gave them were blankets and some food, most importantly we were there to share the love of Christ with them.

After they left, I then turned to my children and said, "You see there, I told you, someone really needed our help."

If only one person would have shown up that afternoon, it was worth braving the cold for. Then I said to my children, "We just gave Jesus a blanket and something to eat."

"Mama, that man with that lady wasn't Jesus was he? How come Jesus didn't have a blanket, Mama?" my baby curiously asked.

Well, I couldn't help from chuckling at their innocent curiosity. So explaining what I really meant, I grabbed my Bible and began to read from the book of Saint Matthew. "Listen to what the Bible says," I told them. Then I began to read to them saying, "Then shall the righteous answer him saying, Lord, when saw we thee an hungered, and fed thee? or thirsty and gave thee drink? When saw we thee a stranger and took thee in? or naked, and clothed thee? Or when saw we thee sick, or in prison, and came unto thee? And the King shall answer and say unto them, Verily I say unto you, Inasmuch as ye have done it unto one of the least of these my brethren, ye have done it unto me."[15]

"You see there, the Bible says, whatever we do for the homeless and the needy, it's just like doing it for Jesus Himself."

After I finished reading the passage, I shut the Bible and closed up Love and Charity for the night. My kids and I walked home, in a spirit of joyous fulfillment, knowing that we were there to assist someone that needed help.

Years had gone by since the first time I asked the Lord for a larger building. During those years, the Love and Charity Club moved to various locations around the Racine area. We were located on two different storefront locations on Main Street. There was also a Washington Street location, and eventually the Douglas Street locations. But in the interim years of transition, the devil launched many more attacks directed at my family and me. Satan tried his best to hinder the work at the Love and Charity Club.

As I mentioned before, he really began to use James to try to discourage me. In 1975 we had just moved the Club to 329 Main Street. By this time James had stopped participating in any of the aspects of the ministry. He just looked for any excuse to leave home, and once he left, we wouldn't see him for days on end. James would always seem to disappear particularly around the holiday seasons when the kids and I needed him the most. He'd always say he had to take some kind of trip or something, but I stayed behind and worked hard helping the others who were in need. When Christmas season would come around, James wouldn't be around to provide for his own family. Ironically, even though we were helping so many other people, we ourselves needed so much help. As my children lay in their beds, Christmas Eve night, I entered into their rooms and I began to weep over them as they slept. My children didn't see me crying that night, and they rarely ever did. But as I stood over them, with tears in my eyes, I began to ask the Lord to help us. I wanted my children to also have a merry Christmas.

"Lord, I don't want anything for myself," I prayed. "I just don't want to see my children go wanting on Christmas Day."

As I petitioned the Lord, he gave me this passage in the Psalms, "...weeping may endure for a night but joy cometh in the morning."[16] So I claimed the victory in Jesus' name and I believed the Lord would be our provider. When Christmas morning came, the Lord had mercy upon us. The Lord put it in people's heart to give to us. People that we knew, as well as those that we didn't know, stopped by with carloads of Christmas gifts. The Lord indeed blessed us with plenty so we all ended up having a very merry Christmas.

Though 1975 had proved to be a good year for Love and Charity, we looked forward to bigger and better things in 1976. You know how it is. There's always a special optimism as a new year begins. My New Year's resolution was, "We are going to help more people than ever before this year." Therefore, with great expectations, we prayed in the new year, during a New Year's Eve "Watch Service." I anxiously looked forward to the new challenges and blessings that 1976 would bring.

As the days and weeks went by, soon the end of February was upon us. It was time for me to make my Widow's Closet home visits. After a hard day's work at the Club, I came home and fed the kids and got them ready for school the next day. Before I left out, I told my seventeen-year-old son Michael to watch the kids while I was gone.

"Y'all behave now, you here! I'll see y'all after awhile," I said.

I left home, anxiously looking forward to doing my home visits. Little did I know the stage for a tragedy was set when I left home that Thursday night, the twenty-sixth of February.

I had made several stops that night, and the time passed by so quickly. It was already after nine p.m., and I was at my last stop. I was visiting a sweet old widowed woman, who just wanted someone to talk to. While I was there, I received a phone call. A friend of mine had tracked me down, to give me some tragic news.

"Mrs. Hunter, there has been a fire at your house tonight. You better come right now. It doesn't look good, Louise," she said sadly.

Not being far from our house, I rushed home the moment I got the news. While I hastily made my way home, the memories of the fire back in Kinson, North Carolina, flashed through my mind. Vivid images of the emergency room and Zoline's burnt body lying limp on the operating table flashed before my eyes. As I ran through the snow and ice, I nearly broke my neck when I slipped and fell. But I quickly got up and continued to press my way through the ice and snow.

As I turned on my street, I could see the reflections of many red emergency lights as they flickered through the smoky night air. The

The killer blaze
Photo by Arthur P. Haas, *Journal Times*, Racine, Wis., 2/27/76

stench of our burning house permeated throughout the entire area. I could hear the noisy sounds of the fire engines, and their radios as they blared out intermittently. I could see firemen scurrying in and out of our burning home. Fire hoses were sprawled out all over the streets and sidewalks. The firemen were spraying relentless streams of water through the second-floor windows. The night sky was illuminated with an eerie reddish-orange light, from the flames that belched up through our rooftop.

As I pressed my way through the crowd of spectators that had gathered outside, I approached one of the firemen and frantically I said, "Sir, this is my home, Where are my babies?"

"Mrs. Hunter, thank God it's you," he replied. "They're all safe. They got out of the house in time, and they're all okay. We're keeping them warm at a neighbor's house," he reassured.

"Take me to them. I want to see my babies now," I insisted.

"OK, Mrs. Hunter, follow me," he replied.

So when I entered my neighbor's house, I saw my poor little children. They were all cuddled up together on the living room couch, covered up in a blanket to keep warm. My youngest girl, Shawn, who was two at the time, began to cry out loud as soon as she saw me walk into the room but my other kids had a nervous type of fright that showed on their faces. They were all very shaken by this tragic ordeal.

Initially, I was relieved to see they were all safe. However, my intuition told me that something was still terribly wrong.

"Hey, wait a minute! All of my children are not here," I shouted.

Now panic-stricken, I desperately began counting my children. The fireman then informed me that they had taken Michael and Paul to the hospital, but it was for minor injuries, nothing life-threatening. I acknowledged what the fireman said, but the Spirit of the Lord kept telling me, *They're not all here!* So this time taking into consideration, Paul and Michael, I counted again.

"No, no, no, somebody's still missing," I shouted. Then it hit me. *Thomas! Where's Thomas?*

"Where's my baby, Thomas? Kids, y'all seen Thomas?" I again exclaimed.

I looked at the fireman and I told him, "Hurry, you must go back into the house. Thomas is not here!"

Immediately the fireman radioed the fire chief and requested them to send the search team back into the house. I left my other children there at my neighbor's and went back to our house. I stood there praying outside of my burning home, hoping that Thomas was still alive. After approximately fifteen minutes, the search team made the announcement over the radio, "We found him! He's alive!"

When I heard that, I sighed a great sigh of relief. They found Thomas in a second-floor bedroom, curled up, in a corner. *Thank you, Jesus*, I sighed. As the fireman hurried Thomas out of the house, I could see

Safe but shocked
Photo by Arthur P. Haas, *Journal Times*, Racine, Wis., 2/27/76

that he had not been burned. However, he was barely breathing and immediately the paramedics placed him on oxygen.

"Looks like smoke inhalation," the attending paramedic informed us. "His pulse is weak and his respirations are shallow. Let's get him to the emergency room right now before we lose him," he insisted.

They closed up the ambulance and quickly sped away to St. Luke's Hospital where he was placed on the critical list. My other son Michael was admitted at St. Mary's Hospital in satisfactory condition after receiving second and third-degree burns and injuries from falling. Apparently, he was forced to jump from a second-story window while attempting to save his brothers from the burning room. Paul was also injured, but he was treated and released from St. Luke's for burns he received to his arm.

According to Paul, a stranger who came out of nowhere rescued him. Apparently, he rescued Paul by rushing into our burning house and placing a large tin can over him, which protected Paul from the deadly flames. Ironically, after this unknown hero risked his life to save my son, he then disappeared into the crowd. We never knew who this man was, and I never got a chance to thank him for saving my son's life.

This tragic blaze, which resulted in the total loss of our home, started when my sons, Thomas, six years old; Paul, five years old; Greg, seven years old; and Tim, eight years old, got a hold of some gas we kept around the house for the lawn mower. Somehow the gas can was knocked over while the boys were playing with matches. Michael was downstairs with the rest of the children. However, when the fire started he tried to rescue all the boys but got trapped by the flames. He ended up having to jump out of the second-story bedroom window to save his own life. I couldn't lay the blame on Michael because he did the best he could. In my eyes, he was a hero because he risked his own life to save his brothers and sisters.

However, though the rest of us survived this tragedy, Thomas was slowly dying back at St. Luke's intensive care unit. Though I travailed and interceded on the behalf of Thomas, on the night of February 27, 1976, my six-year-old baby died from severe smoke inhalation.

These were sad moments in the lives of the Hunter family. It was like dark clouds of mourning that hovered over us all. A part of my life was now gone forever. As much as I had hoped this situation would turn out like it did with Zoline back in Kinson. I was now experiencing the deep agony only a parent can feel when one of their children is taken in a tragedy. I would have given my own life to save my baby. I agonized over the fact that if I had only stayed home that night, none of this would have happened, but it was too late for all that now. Thomas was dead, and no matter how badly I wanted Thomas back, as King David said in the Scriptures, "I can go to him, but he cannot return to me."[17]

After I received the news of my son's death, I had to go and find James who had been gone from home for days. When I finally caught up with him and broke the news, he took it very hard. James came back home with me that night, and both of us tearfully mourned the death of our son together. The next morning, James went to buy himself a black suit to wear to Thomas' funeral. Unfortunately, James would only wear that suit one more time before his own untimely death.

On Friday, March 5, 1976, at 1 p.m., we held the funeral services at the Rose of Sharon Church in Racine. The turnout was tremendous. All of Racine seemed to be there that day. There was standing room only for both the wake and the funeral services. Flowers, cards of condolence, came from everywhere. Many of the people and families that we helped over the years, were all there to pay their respects and mourn with us. Representatives from the mayor's office, as well as from the office of the county executive, were all present. The firemen and police officers that were at the fire also came to pay their respects. There in the sanctuary of the Rose of Sharon Church, we all lamented Thomas' death together.

In the aftermath of this tragedy, the Red Cross provided us with temporary shelter. Additionally, two banks, the Farmer & Merchants' Bank and the M. & I. Bank started trust funds named after Thomas to help us raise money to be relocated. The volunteers from the Love and Charity Club also started a donation drive to replace our destroyed belongings. Also on March 14, the Rose of Sharon Church had a "Louise Hunter Day" to raise funds for our family. The support was overwhelming. People donated furniture, appliances, clothes, food, and money. Soon the Lord had given back to us twice as much of what we'd lost in the fire. And soon we even had another house located on 13th Street. That's where we stayed temporally until we moved on Hamilton Street. Because of all the wonderful support that we received, I called the *Journal Times* and had them release a citywide statement of appreciation. On March 24, 1976, the *Journal Times* ran this statement:

*"We want to express our deepest thanks and gratitude to all of those who helped us in our time of need…No words could never really express our appreciation to all those who have helped us through this ordeal…"*

Although it took me a while to get over the death of my son, I continued to serve the Lord. Over the years I had learned the secret to getting over your own depression and pain, you must reach out to others. If you help someone else while you're hurting, in the process God will heal your pain. When you're busy helping some else, you don't have time to think about your own situation. Therefore, as bad as I was hurting, I never once considered closing down Love and Charity Club. Nor did I blame God for the tragedy because I know that the Lord gives and the Lord takes away.

In time, the fire tragedy was well behind us all, and steadfastly I continued to do the Lord's work. Two long years had passed by, and we were now in the midst of 1978. More and more people volunteered at the Love and Charity Club, so I had all the support that I needed–except that of my husband James. For many nights I lay on the altar in prayer petitioning the Lord on my husband's behalf. I continually asked him to deliver James from that whore-mongering spirit that he had. It would break my heart to see James act such a fool. Like a young schoolboy mesmerized by youthful infatuation and lust, he was being destroyed by his own sinful passions. Though I possessed fortitude and strength, I was still a married woman who needed her husband by her side. And I certainly had the legal and biblical grounds to divorce James, but that's not what I wanted. I forgave James over and over again, desiring to start anew, all because I loved him so much.

It was really hard for me because I was doing such a great work for the Lord. Yet all while I was serving Jesus, my husband was running the streets of Racine. No matter what I said or did, James would not change, and it cast a bad shadow on Love and Charity. People knew who my husband was and his carousing gave the gossipers something to talk about. Late in the night when I lay in my bed alone, James' infidelity tortured me. Although the Lord strengthened me to deal with all the gossips, my heart was broken. No matter who we are, or who we think we are, we're only human and are subject to like passions. You expect your enemies to hurt you, but it's worse when you're hurt by someone you love.

As we approached the Christmas season of 1978, it was a typical Christmas that the Hunter family had unfortunately grown accustomed to. There was no James Hunter to be found. It wouldn't have been so bad, but James would always build the children's hopes up. Each year he would tell them that he was going to buy them Christmas gifts, and each year the kids would look forward to it. They believed James because it's a child's natural inclination to believe what their parents say, especially promises made by their father. My babies were so innocent and forgiving, not knowing that James was going to let them down once again.

In December 1978, James was adamant about going down to Mississippi. This time he wanted to spend the holidays with his mother. When he told me he was going to go, I expected as much. Once again I was the one who would be left behind to face the kids on Christmas day. However, little did I know, the day James left to go to Fayette, Mississippi, to be with his mother, would be the last time that I would see him alive.

Early in the morning on December 30, 1978, I was startled out of a sound sleep when the phone rang. I reached over and picked up the telephone and asked, "Yes, can I help you?"

It wasn't that unusual to get phone calls in the middle of the night because people always called in some kind of crisis. But this time it was James' mother calling long distance from Fayette, Mississippi.

"Louise, it's Elane, (fictional name) James' mother," she said softly.

There was sadness in her voice and her spirit was heavy. She paused for a moment, then said, "Louise, I'm sorry, but I have some bad news. It's about James."

"What kind of bad news?" I asked.

She paused again, then began to sob, saying, "James is dead."

As soon as she said this, it felt like I had been hit in the chest with a brick. In an instant my first reaction was, *This is a bad dream, and in a moment I'll wake up and this will all be gone.* Though this wasn't a dream, it was indeed a living nightmare. It was true. James was dead.

"Oh, my God. What has happened to my husband?" I shouted. "It was a car accident," she replied.

And then she went on to recount the events that led up to James' death, earlier that night. Elane began by saying, James had arrived in Fayette a few days ago. "I was so happy to see him. I hadn't seen him in a couple of years. He seemed to be so happy, just like he didn't have a care in the world. I hadn't seen him so carefree since he was in high school years ago. He was like a jovial young teenager. It really did my heart good to see him so jubilant. I asked, 'How are Louise and the kids? Why didn't you bring them down here with you to see their Grandmama, James? It would have been so nice to see them for the holidays.' He said they were all right and wanted to stay home.

'You know how busy Louise is with that old mission. I couldn't pry that woman away from that place, even if I wanted to,' he insisted. 'Well, I guess you're right son,' I replied. Then James asked me to fix him something to eat. So I did, and we talked some more, but as soon as James ate a little, he jumped right up and got back in that car of his, and from then on, he was in and out, all while he was here.

"The night he died, he was excited about going out with some old girlfriend of his named Elly Mae (fictional name). I told James, that a married man ain't got no business going out with no old girlfriend, but James didn't seem to pay me any mind. Then James said the strangest thing to me. He said, 'Mama guess what? I'm gonna wear my black suit, out tonight.'

"'What black suit, are you talking about?' "I asked.

"'The black suit I bought two years ago to wear to Thomas' funeral mama. I only wore it once, and that was the day we buried him. I guess I just never had the mind to wear it again. But tonight I feel like it's a special occasion, so I'm gonna sport it while I'm out with Elly May,'" he excitedly replied. As I said before, James was in a real good mood when he left last evening. The last thing James said to me was don't wait up for him, cause he'd probably be home in the morning.

"But later that night the sheriff's department called me and told me that James was killed in a car crash. According to the sheriff's account, James was driving down the road and had come to an intersection. There was a truck pulling a trailer home that was also approaching the intersection at the same time. Both vehicles collided in the middle of the intersection. Evidently, the truck driver never saw James' car coming. The truck should have stopped, but it didn't. It smashed broadside into James' car. The sheriff said, James most likely died instantly upon impact."

After she told me all of what had happened the night of James' death, I hung up the telephone and began to weep bitterly. Although James gallivanted around town, and at times was not the best husband, I still loved him so. The last thing I wanted to see was my husband die on some lonely highway miles away from home. If James would have only stayed in Racine, I'm sure he would be alive today.

After coming to grips with the death of a loved one, there's a tendency to hold on to the pleasant memories of the past. Although James and I had been at odds about his behavior, I didn't want to remember him that way. I just wanted to savor the memories of the way things were. I guess how I'd like to remember James could be summed up in this poem.

*Precious memories of the morning we met, in the twilight, star-filled skies.*

*I'll never forget the smile on your face, and the gaze of your big dreamy eyes. Laughing and talking along the way, to toil in the cotton fields.*

*James Hunter's love, revived my heart that pain and rejection had filled.*

*Through years of trials, tribulations and pain together to Racine we came.*

*In search of new life, of hope and dreams, in the land of promise and pain.*

*Yes, there was a time, we worked together and you helped in your own special way, as we proudly stood, you and I*

*on Love and Charity's, opening day.*

*Though I miss you, James, I'll never forget you because I'll always carry your name*

*and I'll continue the work, at Love and Charity in the land of promise and pain....*

So once again dark clouds of mourning hovered over the Hunter family. And again the wings of the death angel cast his melancholy shadows of grief in our hearts. The loss of James Hunter was another very heavy burden for us all to bear. Though unwilling, once again, the Hunters had to walk through the valley of the shadow of death. A path lined with mourning and grief, a path that we must all walk someday. Ironically, even in death, the Lord has the last word. Since I don't believe events in our lives are just mere coincidences, I must share the mysterious facts that surround the deaths of both of my son and my husband. Though they may sound strange, there were some curious similarities between their deaths. Both of their deaths resulted from an accident that occurred on the last Thursday of a winter month. Both had their funerals on the first Friday of the following month. Both had their funeral services at the same church and were eulogized by the same minister. They were both buried in the same cemetery, but the strangest similarity of all was the same black suit that James bought to wear to our son Thomas' funeral two years earlier was the same suit he died in two years later, having never worn that suit again in between time.

# Chapter 7
## Mission Possible

In time, the grief caused by James' tragic death was well behind us all. Yet faithfully I continued to do the work that God had called me to do. At this time Love and Charity was still located at 329 Main Street. One morning after just opening, a man walked in and asked me, "What is this Widow's Closet all about?"

As I was explaining how all this came about, I began to give him my testimony. I went all the way back to how the ministry started in my home years ago. Then I began to explain portions of the vision to him. I told him how I desired a larger facility where I could rehabilitate, the homeless people who came to us for help.

"If we could just get them off of the streets long enough to clean them up and teach them some job skills, they would have a good chance to becoming productive members of society once again," I said.

By the time I was finished talking to him, my passion for the homeless clearly made an impact upon him.

"It really sounds like you're doing a great work here, Mrs. Hunter.

I really wish you all of God's best," he said. "Thank you," I replied.

He then walked out, but no sooner than he left he came right back in and said, "Oh yes, Mrs. Hunter, I do happen to know where there is a property available for rent."

"Where's it located?" I asked.

"It's in the eleven hundred block of Douglas," he replied.

So I thanked him and gave thanks to the Lord for a new lead to follow up on.

A few days after our meeting, I went to see the building the gentleman spoke of. It was a nice property and just the right size. I inquired about renting it. After a short meeting with the owner we reached a rental agreement. To my surprise, the landlord thought using this building for a shelter was a good idea. However, he was asking for two hundred and fifty dollars a month rent. In my mind, I knew it would be tough to make the rent every month, but in my heart I knew this was an answer to prayer. I knew that somehow, some way Love and Charity was about to move into a new home.

This was a big step that I was taking. I knew I couldn't do this alone. I needed as much help as I could get, so I started to rally support from my friends, neighbors and associates, but to my surprise all I met was dissuasion and pessimism.

They were asking questions like, "How you gonna run a homeless shelter without a budget, or grant money? Without money, Louise, you'll never get off of the ground," they claimed. "You don't have the financing, nor the working capital to meet the overhead expenses. Such a venture is ill-advised and bound to fail," they discouragingly said.

I couldn't believe it. The same people that had been willing to help me do other smaller things didn't want to be involved in a greater work. It was as if they could no longer see the point in reaching out to the people that needed help the most.

"Come on, Louise, what's wrong with just keeping the Love and Charity Club, on Main Street?" they asked. "Why do you want to open up a mission for wayward folks? Girl, you don't know what you're getting yourself into. You're a widow. You can't run a mission by yourself," they said.

After all the years I've been taking people in off the streets, why would I turn down the opportunity to open up a mission that would be more effective in meeting the needs of the disadvantaged? Though all these negative comments broke my heart, the Spirit of the Lord began to comfort me. The Lord brought back to my remembrance that the vision was given to me, *not to them*. Therefore, they can never see Love and Charity as I do, because the Lord brought forth Love and Charity out from the womb of *my* innermost being. He gave *me* the faith and the power to accomplish His will. Though people may never understand, God called *me* to do the work, therefore, I was determined not to be detoured by their criticism and pessimism.

Although I didn't have all the moral support that I wanted, I did what David did. I had to encourage myself. I knew if God was for me then who shall stand against me. Therefore, in the face of all the critics and their criticism, I launched out into the deep, and opened up the Love and Charity Mission. Though I didn't know where the rent money would come from, one month to the next, I was fully persuaded that God would supply all of our needs.

For the first time in Love and Charity's history, we now had a building large enough to take in a greater number of the homeless. Though I didn't have any formal education in business administration, nor have I ever directed anything on this scale. The only qualifications I did have was knowing that God had called me to this ministry. Therefore, I was persuaded that He would give me the necessary skill, leadership, and the ability to do the work.

Since I couldn't get encouragement from people, I turned my face to the Lord and searched the Scriptures. In the Psalms, I found a reassuring passage, which says, "Blessed is he that considereth the poor: the Lord will deliver him in the time of trouble. The Lord will preserve him and keep him alive; and shall be blessed upon the earth: and thou wilt not deliver him unto the will of his enemies. The Lord will strengthen him upon the bed of languishing: thou wilt make all his bed in his sickness."[18] From this passage I knew I was doing the right thing. The first people I started to take in were homeless men, and this wasn't easy, to say the least. A lot of these men had some bad habits that were hard to deal with. If a person is homeless, it usually means that they have some serious problems that caused it. Something has to be wrong when a person's own family gives up on them. When people come to Love and Charity for temporary shelter, I had to be very watchful and strict. I learned how to trust my instincts because being too easy in this business could cost you your life. Although the whole purpose of Love and Charity was to help people, there's a thin line between being helpful, and being taken advantage of. Therefore, I had to always use wisdom. It was imperative that I discern whether I was helping a person or being used.

I also relied heavily on some strict rules and regulations that protected the best interests of our residents as well as the staff. Typically, when men would see a woman like me in charge, they automatically tested limits to see what they could get away with. I was often threatened and cursed out. However, I stood firm on the mission's policies trusting that God would deliver me from all harm and danger. Whether they liked it or not, if you're gonna stay here, you must obey the rules. I had to put my foot down on many occasions, either asking them to leave or calling the police when necessary.

Although there are always some bad apples in the bunch, I realized that not everybody that comes to a mission has evil intentions. Many people have had some bad breaks in life. I know, because I have had my share of them, but I always tell my clients that Jesus is the answer, no matter what the situation is.

Since I realized that spiritual interventions play a key role in changing one's life, it was necessary for me to incorporate daily prayer services, as part of the routine here at the mission. If there's one lesson that I learned over the years, it's the importance of prayer. Prayer certainly changes things. We also offered Christian counseling to those who suffered from depression and low self-esteem. This is why we have the Bible studies as well. When people learn to follow biblical principles, they have fewer problems and feel better about themselves. I also found that it's absolutely necessary to meet the needs of the whole man. What this means is to address the issues concerning the mind, the body, and the spirit. This is why I believe Jesus met the physical needs of the people first, then he ministered to their spiritual needs. A person that's well nourished and clothed is in a better position to receive the good news of the Gospel, than someone who is starving and naked. In order to meet the needs of the whole man, many of the local church organizations sent ministers and missionaries to help teach the Bible and preach the Gospel message. It has always been my belief that the Christian community should unite to fight against our common enemy that seeks to destroy neighborhoods and cities.

As the first few weeks in our new building passed by, the money to purchase large amounts of food was not available. I went out to the food stores in town and asked them to help me. I knew that the big food store chains throw away a lot of good food, so I asked them if I could do daily pickups, in order that I might have fresh food to give to the people. Although some rejected us, the Lord gave me favor with some of the biggest food stores in town. This turned out to be a wonderful door of blessing because I received loads of food every day.

Due to the tremendous volume of food that I was now receiving, I ended up with surplus food to give away to families in need. When I gave food to families, I often thought of the real estate woman in Kinson who let me purchase enough food to feed my hungry children. Whenever I gave away food I always thought, *What would I want someone to give me if I needed help today?* So I would gladly give away hefty boxes of food, enough to feed a big family.

As the number of women with children seeking aid from the mission increased, I began to see that many of these families needed shelter as well. I didn't know that there were so many families that were homeless. Although I primarily set up the mission for men, I made room for the families as well. When I had no more space at the mission, I continued taking in families into my own home. Since it's so traumatic to be homeless, I'd always give them my testimony to encourage them not to give up. I knew from experience that Jesus would see them through if they put their trust in Him.

As the scope of the ministry continued to increase, I started up new programs to help meet the needs of the people. Of these new programs, one of them was the hot breakfast program. Every morning I would get up early and come down to the mission to serve breakfast. School children were mostly the ones who enjoyed the program although several adults came to eat breakfast too. The children would be so thankful to eat a hot breakfast before a long day at school. They would often make comments like, "I wish my mama would fix my breakfast each morning."

Whenever those kids made statements like that, it usually indicated that there were some serious problems in the home. When these love-starved children came to Love and Charity, I was the only loving mother image they had. I was the mother image to so many people that the title "Mother Hunter" stuck. Although I had so many of my own children, I didn't mind other folks referring to me as their mother. I remember what Jesus said to one of the disciples, who told him that his mother Mary was seeking him. Jesus asked his disciple, "Who is my mother? Then the Lord said, who does the will of God, the same is my mother..."[19] God had called me to do his will and show love and hospitality to those who came to the mission, so in that sense, I was being a mother to all who came to the mission.

On Wednesday nights I had an open kitchen and served dinner to the public. People would come from all over town, to eat some of my country cooking. Hundreds of people of all races and ages, were fed at Love and Charity each week. I wanted people to be comfortable when they ate at Love and Charity, so I gave our dining facility, a restaurant like atmosphere. The environment in which we serve God's people, should be neat and clean. So often there is a stigma that goes along with the word "mission."

When the average person thinks of a mission they usually think of, an old rundown place, that's musty and full of old dirty men, but I wouldn't have Love and Charity that way. That's where I felt I had an advantage over a man in running the mission. Men usually don't have an eye for creating, a pleasant environment like a woman has. When a person comes to Love and Charity, I wanted that person to be comfortable. One of the golden rules that has always been dear to my heart, is what the Bible teaches, love thy neighbor as thyself [20] which in essence means, do unto others as you would have others do unto you. These are some of the most important commandments that the Bible has given to us. If everyone lived by these commandments our communities, families, and societies would not be in the bad shape that they are in today. The accommodations that I made for others, is what I would like someone else to do for me.

As the time moved on, our first year in the 1131 Douglas Avenue location had passed, and we were now into our second year. The Lord continued to send in the financial donations we needed to stay open. When our finances got low, I was always coming up with ideas to raise funds. Most of the time they were very successful ventures, but there were other times when the bills were due and we didn't have the money. Anonymous donors as well as those that I knew, would send in monetary donations. Sometimes I would get checks for a thousand dollars and more. There would be little notes in the letter that would read: *The Lord put it on my heart, to send you this money. God bless you and continue the good work*. It was completely amazing how God would move on the hearts of Racine's citizens to support Love and Charity.

Instances like these gave me so much encouragement. I realized that I was not in this alone. As it turned out, the experience that I gained at our first Douglas Street location served as stepping stones for where God would be planting us permanently. All our transitional years of trial and error were about to end. There would be no more wandering in the wilderness so to speak. Now I was about to enter into the Promised Land, the place where the Lord had been leading me all the time.

If I were to draw a parallel between my life and the life of a biblical character, Moses would be a good illustration. For example, God had been manipulating circumstances in Moses' life since the very beginning. Although Moses was unaware of this for forty years, God's hand was upon his life leading him every step of the way. After Pharaoh ordered the deaths of all the male Hebrew babies, newly born Moses was also in danger. Since God had a certain purpose for Moses, He prompted his mother to place him in the river to escape certain death. Moses was later plucked from the river by the Pharaoh's daughter who raised Moses as her own son. Being raised in the royal family, Moses was in line to be the Pharaoh of Egypt one day. At the age of forty, Moses received a calling from God that caused him to identify with the plight of his people. Moses forsook the throne of Egypt and the pleasures of sin and began to respond to the calling of God.

Moses, being driven by destiny's call, felt he was to be the deliverer of his people. Therefore, on one occasion he killed an Egyptian that was beating a Hebrew slave. Soon after that incident, Moses saw two Hebrews arguing amongst themselves, so he intervened and saying, "You are brethren. Why fight one another?"

When the two Hebrews heard what Moses had to say, they asked. "Who made you the ruler over us? Will you kill us too, like you did the Egyptian?"

Then Moses had to flee into the wilderness where God's preparation for his ministry lasted for forty more years. When Moses was eighty years old, God revealed himself to Moses in the burning bush. It was only after Moses had been through years of preparations, trials, and tribulations, that God revealed his purpose for his life. Long before Moses' conception it was God's divine master plan at work, which affected every situation and outcome in Moses' life. God was preparing Moses to be a vessel of honor all the time.

Throughout our lives God is molding and shaping us with particular purposes in mind. All the experiences we have in life are not mere coincidences, but are God's unfolding master plans, leading us further down the road to our destiny. It was the same way with my life. In order to have the compassion to serve the needy, I had to experience being needy. In order to encourage those that have suffered rejection, I too had to experience rejection. In order to encourage people to trust God for deliverance, I too needed to experience God's deliverance. In order to comfort the mourners I too, had to suffer the pain of losing a loved one. In order for me to tell the people that God will work a miracle, I had too had experience God's miraculous power.

Through each situation, God's masterful hand was leading and guiding me towards my destiny. Little did I know at the time that the visitations by the nurse, in Vicksburg, and the strange lady in Kinson, would set a precedent in my life. From those experiences, I realized the importance of doing visitations, which became a big part of my ministry. Being burned out of two dwellings and practically evicted out another, provided the basis for me to have compassion on those who need emergency shelter.

For a long time I could not understand the purpose of all these tragic themes in my life. However, in order that we may be yielded vessels unto the Lord, He must take us through trials. Then through experience, we learn that no matter what happens to us in life, "...all things work together for good to them that love God, to them who are the called according to his purpose."[21]

When Love and Charity moved into the 1131 Douglas location, we stayed there for a couple of years. However, God was still calling me to another place. There was something greater that He wanted me to do, somewhere else that he wanted me to be. Though we were doing a great work at the Douglas street location, I had a strange feeling that we wouldn't be there long. Then one day, my hunch was validated when I saw a beautiful building right down the street from where we were.

One block south on Douglas Street, there was a nice building that had a for sale sign on in. It was much lager that our current building and was better suited for a mission. As I looked at it, I wanted it, and that's when the Lord spoke to my heart saying, "It's yours. Go and claim it."

So one morning I got up and the Spirit of the Lord spoke to my heart again and said, "The walls shall come down."

At first, I didn't understand what the Spirit was telling me. Soon I understood that there would be walls of resistance that could hinder Love and Charity's move into that building.

So as I pondered about the situation, I remembered what Joshua did when faced with the walls of Jericho. So in faith, I walked over to Prospect Street, believing that God was going to give me the victory.

When I reached the corner of Prospect and Douglas Street, where this building was located, the Spirit of the Lord said to me again, "The walls shall come down."

So in faith, just like Israel was commanded to march around Jericho seven times, I did the same. I marched around the perimeter of this building seven times, praising and giving glory to God. After the seventh time, I stopped at the corner of Prospect and Douglas and laid hands on this building, and claimed it for Love and Charity in the name of Jesus. To those driving down Douglas Street that morning, I must have been a strange sight to see, but then again Israel must have looked silly to Jericho's army when they saw the nation of Israel marching around their supposedly impregnable walls. Israel was a peculiar nation and a peculiar people, and so it is with me, I am most peculiar and I know it.

According to the Bible, Christians are supposed to be a peculiar people. When the world looks at us, they should be able to see that we are different from them. We also fight our adversaries differently as well. As the Scriptures say, "For though we walk in the flesh, we do not war after the flesh. For the weapons of our warfare, are not carnal, but mighty through God to the pulling down of strongholds."[22]

When I was marching around that building that's exactly what I was doing. I was pulling down strongholds of resistance. After I finished marching and praying, I took down the telephone number written on the for sale sign. I called the number and asked to speak to someone about this property. To my surprise, it was owned by the Cristo Rey Parish which was a local Hispanic Parish, here in Racine. I told them that I was Louise Hunter of Love and Charity, and that I was interested in renting the property on 1031 Douglas Ave.

Ironically, it seemed like the first form of resistance that I encountered was being placed on hold for several minutes. However, while

I was on hold, I began to pray, asking God to go before me and clear all hindrances out of the way. When the receptionist returned to the line she said, "I'm sorry, Mrs. Hunter, we are only interested in selling the property, not renting it out."

"O.K., thank you," I replied.

I then hung up the telephone. Although I didn't get the answer that I wanted, I refused to be discouraged. I thought of Moses when he first went to Pharaoh to get him to let Israel go, of course Pharaoh said no, and hardened his heart. Moses remained faithful to what God had told him, and that's the same thing that I did. I remained faithful to what God had told me. I believed in my heart that the building was mine. Over all these years, God hadn't failed me yet, and I knew He wasn't going to fail me now.

So as the months went by, occasionally I would call the Christo Rey Parish, to see if someone had purchased the building yet. The answer was still no, but then the receptionist said something that encouraged me and let me know that there was still hope. The receptionist informed me that many people had looked at the building, but no one seemed to want it. Then she said, "We're having an unusually hard time trying to sell this building and none of us understand why."

When I heard that, I knew it was the Lord's hand at work. They didn't realize it, but the building couldn't be sold to anyone else. It had already been claimed in Jesus' name, for Love and Charity. Therefore, no one else *could* buy it.

After a little more time had elapsed, I called the parish again. However, this time they said that they wanted to talk to me. So we set up an appointment to meet that afternoon. When the appointed time came, I went to meet with them as scheduled.

As I sat down to speak to one of the parish officials, he began to tell me how they'd been having a difficult time selling the property. Then he said, "Frankly, Mrs. Hunter, we can't seem to sell it. Prospective buyers come and look at it, but they don't want to buy it. We've got to do something with the building because it's costing us money to maintain it. So Mrs. Hunter, our board of directors has decided to go ahead and let Love and Charity rent the building."

When he said that, I was elated. The walls had finally come down indeed. Now Love and Charity could go occupy the building. It was a wonderful victory that the Lord had won for us.

Though they agreed to let us have use of the building, there were still some obstacles to overcome. For example, coming up with the two hundred and fifty dollars a month rent at 1131 Douglas, was a struggle by itself. However, the rent for this building was even higher. In addition to this, the building was much larger than our current location, which meant the overhead expenses would be costlier. But I was confident that as the Lord had been providing all these years, He would faithfully continue to do so.

So after all the papers were signed and everything else was finalized, we moved Love and Charity into its new home. Although moving was quite an arduous task, our work had really just begun. This 6,892 square foot building needed a lot of work. It needed a new roof, electrical work, plumbing, painting, and lots of carpentry work.

To the undiscerning eye, this building looked as if though it was not worth all the trouble to repair it, but I saw this building like a jeweler sees an uncut diamond. When looking at an uncut diamond, the diamond cutter envisions the beauty inside the crude stone. He then applies his masterful skill to bring out all its beautiful hidden characteristics. When he's finished, the crude stone has been transformed into a beautiful gem.

This building was my diamond in the rough. It would take vision and skill to bring the beauty out of this precious stone. After a couple of months in our new building, the monetary donations only trickled in. The small amount of financial support was simply not enough to keep our bills current. Our gas bill was already beginning to mount and coupled with other operating expenses such as the rent, the load was getting heavy, so I stayed in constant prayer about the situation, but there was no relief in sight.

One month, I really became concerned after we failed to pay our rent on time. As much as I had seen God do in the past, I was concerned and needed help in this current situation. After all, we live from faith to faith. However, I'm no different from anyone else who's under a lot of stress. Faith or not, I'm still human, and there are times when I have been worried, but oh how God came through for Love and Charity!

That following Monday morning after waking up and getting prepared for another long day at the mission, I looked out of the window saw thick gloomy clouds in the sky. *Looks like it's going to rain today*, I thought. I turned on the radio and got the weather report, and as I expected, the weatherman confirmed what I could already see. However, it turned out to be worst than what I thought because the forecast was for severe thunderstorms moving into the area later that afternoon.

Later on that day it began to rain. I mean it really began to rain. It was an awful thunderstorm with high winds, hail, and torrents of rain. It reminded me of that terrible thunderstorm when the plane crashed years ago back on our farm. Ever since then, severe storms have always been unsettling to me. When this storm was finally over, there had been a record amount of rain that had fallen that afternoon. As it turned out, the storm had also wreaked havoc at Love and Charity. The rainwater poured through our deteriorating roof and flooded out the mission. It was a real mess and; I was disgusted and discouraged. This flood only added to the problems that we already were having with the building.

After walking throughout the building, assessing the damage, I went to check the basement. When I opened up the basement door and looked downstairs I couldn't believe my eyes. The run off water from Prospect Street had flooded the entire basement. Water seemed to be waist deep.

"Oh no! My God what I'm I going to do now?" I cried. It was a complete mess down there.

It was at this point, it was like I could hear the devil laughing. *You should have never moved in here*, my conscience taunted.

In an instant, I recalled all my critics' comments, and every negative thought flooded my mind. I almost fell into a pit of despair. However, I shook myself and began to focus on how to fix this problem. I got on the phone and called the owners to get them out here to look at the flood damage. Within an hour or so, the Cristo Rey Parish sent over some of their representatives to assess the damage. After they saw it, they seemed to be at a loss for words.

However, I got the strange impression that this wasn't the first time that this building's basement had been flooded.

"Will this happen every time it rains hard?" I asked.

"Well, it's been a problem over the years, Mrs. Hunter," the gentleman replied.

"Well, what can be done about it? I use this basement to store my furniture and other mission supplies. As you can see, everything down here is either damaged or completely ruined," I insisted.

"Mrs. Hunter, I'm sorry we'll have to get back to you on this," he replied.

So after they left, I took this situation to the Lord in prayer.

A few days later I received a telephone call from a parish representative. The man on the phone said, "Mrs. Hunter, unfortunately, we don't have the money in our budget to replace any damaged items in the basement, but if you will get the water out of the basement and fix up the building, we are going to let Love and Charity stay there rent free, and we'll even keep up the liability insurance on the building."

When I heard this, I was absolutely ecstatic. "Yes, that will be fine. We'll have the basement cleared out in no time," I replied. When I hung up the telephone, I began to praise God aloud, shouting, "Hallelujah, it's a miracle. Thank you Jesus!"

The mission was filled with my jubilation, as I offered up the sacrifice of praise unto the Lord. Just as it was in Noah's day, the same rains which destroyed the wicked also delivered Noah and his family. It was just like that for the Love and Charity Mission. God sent the rain to deliver Love and Charity, from some financial burdens that the mission was under. Right when the enemy wanted us to be discouraged, God gave us this awesome victory.

What a mighty God we serve! In my wildest dreams I could have never imagined that God would open up the windows of heaven and send a flood, to wash away my debt and tears. Tell me who wouldn't serve a wonderful God like that?

For the next five years, the Love and Charity Mission would stay in that building, rent free. I thank God for answering my prayers the way he did. So often we will ask God to change our situations, but God often changes the circumstances that affect our situations. The storm that occurred on that gloomy Monday afternoon may have wreaked havoc for others in Racine County, but for Love and Charity Mission, it was nothing short of a miracle.

Once we had gotten over the rent issue, it seemed as if though the Lord sent in a whole new wave of faithful supporters. It was just as God's word says, "Cast your bread upon the waters: For thou shalt find it after many days."[23] Once again the Lord proved to be faithful to His Word. The blessings that I had cast upon the waters were now returning to Love and Charity upon wave after wave. In the following years, we continued to receive small contributions from private citizens as we always have. However, we also began to receive large donations from well-established organizations.

One these companies was Racine's own Johnson Wax Corporation, which gave us thousands of dollars to continue the renovation work at the mission. Another very important donation that we received was from the 700 Club. This nationwide ministry directed by Pat Robertson, sent us two hundred and fifty dollars a month for over two years. Other local contributors, who also gave us generous monetary contributions were the: Racine Police Department's Benevolent Association, the Racine Foundation, the Racine Goodfellars and various other church organizations and social groups. Large grocery stores like Pick-N-Save, and Save U, continued to give large amounts of produce, meats, and bakery products. Through the gracious donations of businesses and merchants of Racine, we continued to feed hundreds of disadvantaged citizens each week.

Since there was also a lot of remodeling work to be done at the mission, construction companies, and contractors started donating some of their services as well. Through their efforts, this old hulk of a building was being transformed into a wonderful place for the homeless. Just as the crude diamond must be cut and shaped to bring out its beauty, so was Love and Charity beginning to take on a beautiful new shape. Soon carpenters were coming in regularly enough to get Love and Charity's chapel finished. The local churches donated pews, benches, and pulpit furniture. Additionally, music stores donated organs, pianos, guitars, and drums. Other Christian organizations brought in all kinds of literature, such as Bibles, hymnals and Sunday School books. The furniture stores also did their part by donating chairs, and tables and couches. A prominent businessman, who also wanted to do his part, purchased the beautiful carpeting that we have in our chapel.

It really blessed my soul when Love and Charity's chapel was completed. In this hallowed chapel, the homeless and the needy could worship the Lord in the beauty of Holiness. Men and women, boys and girls could come here to give their lives to Jesus. In our chapel, we could give praise to His name as long and as loud as we wanted to. To help beautify the chapel, I had two large glass block crosses installed, so the sunlight could illuminate the services while we worshiped. One of the local bricklayers, a very nice young man, volunteered to install both crosses for us. I told him to place the crosses on opposite sides of the wall, right behind the pulpit. When the sun shines through those crosses, it puts me in mind of God's beautiful Shechinah glory. For me, these crosses stand as a memorial to the victory that Jesus has given us here at Love and Charity. They remind me of how we overcame so many adverse situations.

Yes, that old rugged cross is the emblem of suffering and pain, triumph and victory, death and life eternal. For without the preaching of Calvary's Cross, the Gospel is just another story, and Jesus is just another man and Love and Charity is just another mission. But the cross separates Jesus from all other men. Therefore, the cross is a victorious sign for all those that believe.

As things began to shape up around Love and Charity, I began taking in more and more homeless men. My experience with them at 1131 Douglas location really paid off. I already had a well-established reputation as a no-nonsense woman who ran the mission with a rod of iron. In order to maintain control I had to have strict rules. To curb down on admitting undesirables, I did most of the intake screening interviews myself. Since I am the mother of twenty-one child (nineteen who are living) I know almost every trick in the book. I could look right into a person's eyes as they talked to me, and I could tell if they were being honest or not. Using my woman's intuition, I could tell when things were not right about a person. It always amazed me to hear all the different stories that people would give as the reasons why they're homeless. To let them tell it, it was always somebody else's fault. Usually the minute someone starts blaming others for their situation, it raises a red flag that I'm not getting the whole story.

During the intake interview, I would always lay down the mission rules. I'd make sure that they understood them, so there wouldn't be any misunderstandings. I would tell them that if they were going to stay at the mission, they had to take a shower, and get into some clean clothes if necessary. I also told them that I had a seven p.m. curfew, and they had to attend chapel services and prayer.

To prevent the men from being idle during the day, I required them to work around the mission. I didn't think three or more hours of chores was being unreasonable especially when you consider that I work twelve to sixteen hours a day, cleaning up, cooking the meals, and doing the pickups. Besides it was important for me to keep them busy, because as the saying goes, *an idle mind is the devil's workshop*. It is too easy to be tempted to do wrong when people sit around doing nothing. Therefore, I put them to work because work is good. It keeps people occupied and gives them purpose. This is how much of the renovation work around the mission was actually done, by the residents that stayed at Love and Charity.

Whether it's doing work around the mission, or attending prayer and worship services, all this works together to rebuild our clients' lives. Love and Charity was not merely a homeless shelter, or just a place to get a meal. It was a place where a person could reshape their entire character, so they could go on to lead productive lives. I like to think of the mission as a *filling station*. People, who are on their way somewhere else, can stop in and fill up on whatever they need, and then go on their way. We were here to assist them in the transition from being homeless to independent. When we could, we'd help them find employment. If a person leaves the mission cleaned up and reformed but has no income, the chances are, sooner or later, they will be returning to the mission, so before a person leaves Love and Charity, I want them to be saved, cleaned up and fully employed.

One day I took in a man named Dale Bowers who was from out of town and needed a place to get situated. When I interviewed him, he told me he was out of work, out of money, and had nowhere to stay. I felt a deep sense of compassion for him, and I really wanted to help him. I told him to stay here at the mission for a while and give the Lord a chance to work things out in his life. He agreed to stay for a while and he promised he would work hard to make a change in his life. That same evening he gave his life to Jesus during the worship service. I was very happy for him. From that moment on, I saw something special in him, something that I liked.

Dale turned out to be a great help to me at Love and Charity. He was hardworking and very dependable. We really worked well together. Dale had a sincere desire to help me run Love and Charity, which was so important to me. I appreciated those who had a willing heart and mind to help out around the mission. Dale also demonstrated the ability to run things while I was gone. For once, I could leave the mission and know things were in the right person's hands while I was away. As time moved on, we began to spend more time with one another. Soon it became obvious that Dale was growing very fond of me. As a rule I normally don't get personally involved with the mission men. It's not wise because some will try to take advantage of you, while others won't respect you, but with all of this in mind, I broke my own rule and Dale and I became close friends.

It wasn't long after that I began to feel those old flames of passion igniting inside me once again. It was wonderful. The emotions and desires for a man that I'd kept buried inside for so long now were now suddenly coming alive once again. Dale's love was just what I needed in my life at the time. I really needed someone that I could open up to. Just as the sunrise beckons the flowers to open each day, so had the light of love caused my heart to open up to Dale Bowers. The passions that I had locked away in the chambers of my heart were now free to blossom and grow. Once again I was in love, and it felt so good. I no longer tried to hide my feelings behind thin veils of denial.

There was certainly some controversy that circulated about Louise Hunter and that mission man, Dale Bowers. People have talked about me for all of my life, so I wasn't concerned about it now. The fact was, Dale, and I had fallen in love. After knowing Dale Bowers for only six months, for the second time, I exchanged wedding vows, and I became Louise Hunter-Bowers. I would have never guessed that my future husband would walk through the doors of Love and Charity seeking help. While Dale was just looking for a place to lay his head for the night, he ended up finding himself a new life, and a wife as well. It was like a dream, just too good to be true. Yet that was the very problem, because it wasn't a dream, and it was *too good* to be true.

One thing that I've learned over the years is, whenever the Lord gives us a victory or blesses us, the devil always counter attacks. Although Satan could never get me to stop serving the Lord, he always seemed to attack me through my loved ones. Dale and I had been married now for two years, but towards the end of that time period, things between us had begun to change. First of all, my older children never really accepted Dale, particularly since he was once a mission man. They were understandably suspicious, and that caused somewhat of a problem between us. The kids didn't want to mind a man that was not their natural father. During this period, some of my boys, were getting involved with drugs, alcohol, and gangs. My daughters were every bit as promiscuous as I was, and they too were having children at young ages. Considering all that was going on around us, the stress was building on everyone. Not only were the domestic situations troubling Dale, but the day-to-day pressures of running the mission started to wear on him.

By this time, donations had fallen off considerably. The 700 Club had stopped sending their monthly donations, so we were once again faced with a lot of pressure with fundraising, and other important business matters. For some reason, that I couldn't put my finger, Dale was becoming more distant and increasingly withdrawn. Then he started to complain that I wasn't spending enough time with him. He blamed the mission for taking all of my time away from him. Then Dale began to ask questions like, "What's more important, this mission or me?" He would also make statements like, "If you really loved me you would spend more time with me."

What Dale failed to realize is, I was serving Jesus, through thick and thin, long before he came along. He had no right to place himself between the mission and me. He seemed to have forgotten, that if it wasn't for Love and Charity, when he was hungry, he would not have had a place to eat. If I wouldn't have taken him in, he would not have had anywhere to lay his head that night. If it were not for Love and Charity, he would not have found himself a blessed wife that loved the Lord.

None of these things seemed to make a difference to Dale, and one day Dale and I had a serious talk. Dale said, "Louise, I'm sick of this mission. Day in and day out, it's the same old thing. Pickups, donations, worship services, fundraisers, and all these bills. I'm tired of this, and I just can't take it anymore. Let's get away from here, Louise, away from all the pressure and this old mission that's tearing us apart. Come on, baby, What do ya say? Think about it," he pleaded.

Well, I couldn't believe my ears. The audacity of him to ask me such a thing, I was absolutely appalled. Then I said, "Dale, for you to ask me to walk away from this mission is just like you asking me to walk away from Jesus. You know something, I walked away from the Lord, once before, many years ago, but I'll never do it again, because the Lord has been too good to my family and me. No, I will never leave this mission. Love and Charity was birthed from my own womb as though it were one of my own children. I labored with it. I suffered for it. I prayed and fasted for it. I went hungry and did without for it, and I will die first before I walk out and forsake it. My whole purpose in this life is to bless God's people, and you're asking me turn my back on that! Dale Bowers, it will be over my dead body," I angrily responded.

After hearing me, Dale had become angry. Disgust was written all over his face. Then he uttered these words to me saying, "Louise, it's either me, or this mission, one or the other, you can not have us both. So help, me God, Louise, I will leave here and never turn back!"

When Dale said that, then I responded in a stern tone, "Then God will have to help you then, Dale Bowers, because I will not forsake this mission, today or any other day. If it means our marriage, or if it means my life, so be it. I will not forsake the work that God has given me to do, and that's all I got to say about it. You walked in here by yourself, and that's the way you'll walk out of here," I retorted.

I'll never forget the day that Dale gave me that ultimatum. My heart ached for him, but I wasn't about to submit to Dale's dictates. He didn't realize that Satan was manipulating him to get me to forsake the work that God called me to do, nor did he realize that I'm a true servant of the Lord. I don't serve just to please people. I serve to please the Lord. It's just like what the Bible says, "For do I now persuade men or God? Or do I seek to please men? for if I yet please men, I should not be the servant of Christ."[24]

The next morning, without so much as one word between us, Dale Bowers packed up his belongings and left Racine. Once again I had found myself abandoned by the man that I loved, but this time I wasn't shattered like I was years ago when Percy Jones deserted me. This time my heart was fixed, and I held on to Jesus. Yes, it hurt a little, because I'm only human, but Dale forced me to choose between him and Jesus Christ. Needless to say, it was no contest.

After Dale left me, I didn't hear from him for a long time. Then one day about a year later, Dale called me at the mission. When I picked up the telephone I was surprised to hear from him.

"Hi, how are you?" he asked.

"I'm okay. Who is this?" I inquired. "This is Dale, Louise," he responded.

After hearing him I was shocked because he sounded different. He wasn't the vivacious Dale that I was accustomed too. "Dale, how are you? I haven't heard from you in such a long time now."

"I know, Louise. After leaving that morning, I couldn't get myself to call you no sooner than now. I'm sorry about that," he replied. Then he went on to say, "Louise, I'm really sorry that I walked out on you last year. You deserved better than that from me. After all, if it were not for Love and Charity and you, I would not have gotten as far as I did, but I just couldn't continue to live a lie any longer."

"What do you mean by that Dale?" I asked.

"Louise, you're a good woman, and you're doing a great work for

God there in Racine. You deserve a good man, someone who can work with you in the ministry, and that, could have never been me, Louise," he explained.

"But, Dale, you were such a great help to me. I thought we worked well together," I replied.

"No, Louise, I was hiding something from you. I wasn't as committed to the mission as I let on, and I started drinking again. I was just playing a role, Louise. I was never really committed to the mission or to the Lord. I just wanted you so badly. You were everything I thought that I needed in life, and I figured that once we were married, I could finally change. I realized that I couldn't do it. So you see, Louise, that next morning after we talked, I made a decision to go back to the life I once knew, and that's the real reason why I left. I'm so sorry that I hurt you. Would you please forgive me?" he sincerely asked.

Finally, Dale went on to say that he would go ahead and give me a divorce, and would also pay for all the legal proceedings. He also promised to call the judge and tell him that the divorce was no fault of mine. Dale insisted that he take the entire blame. So not long after that, Dale Bowers and I were legally divorced.

Looking back on it, both Dale and I made serious mistakes. First of all, I should have never listened to my emotions. If I had only sought the Lord, I would have heard from Him, and would not have been deceived. The fact is, God knew that Dale wasn't being sincere, but I didn't know.

Dale's mistake was thinking that marriage would change things for him. An addiction is a serious thing that you can't just cover up. Not even marriage can break the chains of alcoholism. You must be delivered from such a thing. A person must have the desire to want to change for themselves.

After this experience with Dale, I'm much more careful. I don't get too close to our clients. The reason why is that the mission men are here today and gone tomorrow. Besides, we know very little about these people's backgrounds and vices. As I have often said, Love and Charity is not a church. People don't come here to join and become members like you do at a church. Love and Charity is like a filling station where those who have needs can get what they need and then move on.

Although I will love our residents with the love of the Lord, and will help them all I can, I'm not here to make friends. I'm here to serve Jesus by providing a place of refuge and hope to those that have fallen on hard times.

After the divorce from Dale was finalized, other problems started popping up. To our consternation, the Cristo Rey Parish, which was under the auspices of the Milwaukee Archdioceses, informed us that we could no longer occupy the building rent free. We were also informed that parish could no longer continue to foot the bill for the buildings liability insurance. As a result of these sudden cut backs, these financial burdens shifted onto our shoulders. In view of this, I became very concerned. It had been five long years that we had received the benefits of their grace, but now without warning we were suddenly faced with a staggering financial load.

As I began to pray about this situation, the Spirit began to minister to me. He brought back to my memory that the Lord had already given this building to Love and Charity, so I had to stay focused on the vision and not the financial problems. As I waited on the Lord, what appeared to be another set of hindering circumstances was actually another avenue of blessing. If they can't let us stay here for free any longer, then maybe they'll sell us the building. Since I wanted to be a good steward over the financial donations that the Lord was sending us, I would rather purchase the building than rent it, anyway.

The question was, if they sell it to us, how much will they sell it for, and where will the money come from? The banks aren't interested in how much faith you have. They want to see dollars. So I decided to call a meeting of my associates to discuss fund raising alternatives.

In early 1987, by joint consensus we decided it would be in our best interest, to appoint a board of directors to oversee any fund-raising campaigns. That meant we would have to incorporate and hold an election to appoint a board of directors. We also have to set up a corporate account with one of the local banks to hold any funds that were raised. Now the next question was what kind of fund-raising drives should be implemented to raise the operating capital? As we brainstormed to come up with some practical ways to raise money, we entertained a hundred or so ideas, ranging from bake sales, to fund raising banquets.

There were a lot of issues to deal with in these meetings. Therefore, they could be quite taxing at times. Often I came away from these meetings mentally fatigued and drained. I was never really good at administrative and formal matters which is why I eventually chose highly skilled professionals to be on my board of directors.

A few days later, I received a call from Mr. Munson, one of our board members. He informed me that the Milwaukee Archdiocese was giving us an option to buy the property from them for a very reasonable price. So I asked him, "How much do they want for it?"

"Thirty thousand," he replied. "That's a good price?" I asked. "Yes, Louise, it is. It's fifteen thousand dollars below what the building actually appraises for," he replied.

So I said, "Tell them yes. We'll take it," I replied.

At last we were finally taking steps toward ownership of the building. As God began opening doors for us to purchase the property, the vision was becoming much clearer. He was bringing the desires of my heart to pass in such a magnificent way because the years of transition were over. The trials, mistakes, and victories that we experienced during those transitional years were in preparation for the place God had prepared for us. Now that we would be planted in a permanent location, our roots could grow deep and the ministry could flourish, all to the glory of God.

In October 1987, we elected our first official board of directors, and Mr. James Hamilton was our first president. I felt that the Lord had really blessed us because Mr. Hamilton was the president of the Green Corporation, a major sub-contractor to Case International Harvester. I felt Mr. Hamilton would make a good president because he knew all about administration, banking, and financing. He was also a very generous man, who donated land to the mission where we eventually built our dining facility years later. During the election process, we also elected four additional officers and ten auxiliary members for a total of fifteen board members. Now that we had an official board of directors we could focus on purchasing the building from the Milwaukee Archdiocese. However, while they were busy having meetings and planning fund raising functions, I was on my knees in prayer. Though we now had a very qualified board, I still sought divine direction on how to raise the thirty thousand dollars needed to purchase the building.

As I stated earlier, I would usually hear from the Lord early in the mornings while taking my bath. There in my relaxing bath water, there were no distractions. In this blessed quietness, I could hear from the Lord. Softly, He would speak to my heart and give me directions on which way I should go. Such was the case the morning the Lord showed me how to raise the thirty thousand dollars. The Lord led me to do two things. The first was to call up the *Journal Times* and have them run an article asking twenty-eight people to donate one thousand dollars each. The second was to start a penny drive. A penny drive. What a simple yet brilliant way to appeal to the public.

So in obedience to the Lord, I called the *Journal Times* and gave them all the necessary information. In the next few days, the newspaper sent a photojournalist out to Love and Charity to get the story and to take pictures. That next morning there it was in the newspapers, *"Three million pennies buy homeless a home."*

Photo by Chuck D'Acquisto, *Journal Times*, Racine, Wis., 9/1/87

I couldn't believe it, the idea that the Lord had given me to announce a penny drive was the headline of the article. And the response to the article was great.

## A Wonderful Gift

Within a short period of time, thousands of dollars flooded into the mission. But the most touching aspect of this fund raiser was the children that participated in the penny drive. They brought pennies to the mission, in cups, jars, boxes, bags, and their own cute little piggy banks. God had moved on the hearts of some of Racine's children to help buy a home for Racine's homeless. Yes, Racine's little ones turned out to be a great example for the adults. It's just like what the word of God says, and a little child shall lead them.[25]

In January 1988, the *Journal Times* ran the story that Love and Charity had an agreement with the Milwaukee Archdiocese to purchase the building for thirty thousand dollars. In the agreement, we had to come up with a ten thousand dollars down payment by January 31. We were able to work out a financing agreement which was a three hundred dollars a month, no interest mortgage payment, that was to be spread out over a seven-year period.

With only days before the deadline, we were still twenty-five hundred dollars short of the ten thousand dollars we needed for the down payment. Therefore, we mobilized all our resources to reach our goal. Phone calls were made, pledges collected, friends and associates contacted. Everyone got involved. And as a result of the tireless collective efforts of our board members and volunteer staff, we were able to reach our twenty-five hundred dollar objective just in time. Since we received financial support from so many organizations, this campaign could no longer be considered just another Louise Hunter-Bowers project. This was indeed a collaborative community effort and a victory for the entire city of Racine.

By August 1988, Love and Charity had raised over thirty-two thousand dollars. This was a real blessing because the mission has always run on a, hand-to-mouth, shoe-string budget, but now we finally had some financial stability. With our new board of directors in place, we could effectively oversee our expenditures and set reasonable financial goals. Although our treasure chest was fuller than it had ever been, our financial burdens were not over by a long shot. Since we had some working capital, we were able to pay off the ten thousand dollar down payment, purchase insurance and settle utility bill debts. After clearing these financial hurdles, we only had about twenty thousand dollars left in our war chest. However, eight thousand dollars of that was designated to repair our roof, which was a big drain on our resources.

It's strange but the leaking roof and the flooding basement were actually the catalyst that opened the door for us to get the property in the first place. After we began to purchase the building, then God supplied the money to fix that old leaky roof, so you see it all worked out, anyway. This is why I try to encourage God's people, because the Bible says, "Be anxious for nothing, but in everything by prayer and supplication, with thanksgiving let your request be made known to God. And my God shall supply all your needs according to His riches in glory in Christ Jesus."[26] So every day of my life, by faith, I continue to look to the Lord to keep this mission functional. As it says in the Psalms, "I will lift up my eyes unto the hills, whence cometh my help. My help cometh from the Lord, which made heaven and earth."[27]

## Chapter 8
### Remembrances

Looking at the world around us, norms and ethics are constantly being redefined. In today's society there is an increasing amount of opposition to biblical principles. We live in a world that seems to have no sense of moral values, nor even acknowledges that there is a God. Observing this, one might ask, What good does it do to live righteously? And what's the purpose of believing in or even serving God? It seems as if though those who live outside the will of God, are getting ahead in life, anyway. At one time or another many of you that are reading this book may have asked these questions. What good does it do? That's an age-old question that God's people have asked for centuries.

The truth is, when serving the Lord, initially there may be no visible results or obvious benefits. By using an illustration drawn from farming we might extract some useful information and instruction to help us cope with this seeming inconsistency. It's just like a farmer that plants seeds in his field hoping for a prosperous crop. For the first few months, he sees no results of his labor. However, in due season a crop springs forth which yields a great increase and bears witness to God's favor.

In the book of Malachi, Israel asked the same question. What good is it to serve the Lord? And the Lord answered and said, "Then they that feared the Lord spake often one to another: and the Lord hearkened, and heard it, and a book of remembrance was written before him for them that feared the Lord, and thought on his name. And they shall be mine, saith the Lord of the host, in that day when I make up my jewels; and I will spare them as a man spareth his own son that serveth him."[28] The Lord has prepared a book of Remembrance for those who serve and Love him. He will not forget our labor of love.

Though our sacrifices may seem to go unnoticed, the Bible gives us a different perspective. As it states in the book of Hebrews, "For God is not unrighteous to forget your work and labor of love, which ye have shewed toward his name, in that ye have ministered to the saints and do minister."[29]

As the Bible so clearly proclaims in this passage, God is not so oblivious to our commitments that he would forget the labor of love that we show toward His name, and toward His people. One day those of us that have suffered for Jesus shall also reign with him. Those of us that have sown righteousness in his kingdom, shall reap our eternal reward of glory. Those of us that have presented ourselves as living sacrifices will hear the Lord say to us, Well done, my good and faithful servant…Enter thou into the joy of thy Lord.[30]

While serving the Lord here at Love and Charity, I have had my share of pain and suffering over the years. As I have walked this road of faith, I've had many experiences that I will always cherish. Although there have been setbacks and losses, there have also been many glorious victories that pale the setbacks and misfortunes. These are the treasured memories of the men and women, the boys and the girls, whose lives have been transformed here at Love and Charity. As I reminisce those precious moments, and look back at it, like an epiphany, it suddenly all made sense. Knowing that the hungry have been fed, the naked clothed, and the homeless sheltered, brings great joy and fulfillment to my life. While I was in this midst of my trials and tribulations, I yet reached out to others.

When I was burdened with a broken heart, I consoled others who were hurting. I didn't have the time to think about my own pain because I was too busy comforting someone else. By being a blessing to other people, I was really being a blessing to myself. Therefore, I was made better by those experiences and I am strengthened and encouraged by their memories.

The Love and Charity Mission itself stands as a memorial to what the Lord can do, how He is able to make a way out of no way. I shall ever forget the miracles of His amazing grace that He performed right here at Love and Charity. Not only in the lives of my own family, but God has made a difference in the lives of so many others as well. Although I'm not God, and I certainly can't reward anyone, it would also be unrighteous for me to forget all the precious people that God has sent through this mission. They are forever etched on the tablets of my heart. They are truly my most cherished remembrances.

Over the years here at Love and Charity, in one way or the other, thousands of people have been helped. Out of the vast majority of these, most are very grateful for what we have been able to do for them. But one would be quite surprised at the number of those that have never even returned to say thank you. It reminds me of a passage of Scripture found in St. Luke, concerning the ten lepers that Jesus healed. As the Lord was approaching from a distance, they all begged for His mercy. So the Lord having compassion on them all, told them, "Go show yourselves unto the Priest." So as they went on their way to the temple, they were all miraculously healed.

After a little while, one of the cleansed lepers returned to the Lord and gave God the glory. He fell down at His feet and worshiped Him for the miracle that He performed. But then the Lord asked, "Were there not ten that were cleaned? Where are the nine?"[31] You would think that they would have shown their gratitude for the Lord's mercy. But as it was in this story, so it is today. People can be self centered and too quick to forget the grace of God. Therefore, it's always a pleasure when someone returns to show their gratitude. Therefore, it is my pleasure to share the story of a man who thought he tried everything, until he came to Love and Charity.

## Share Your Prayer

In July 1986, an elderly man came to the mission seeking a place to lay his head for the night. His face was flush, his expression was distraught, and he staggered a little as he walked into the mission. I told him to be seated and then I asked him if I could get him a cup of coffee or something. He said that he would indeed like a cup of coffee. So after I served his coffee, I began to interview him. "What's your name, sir?" I asked.

Then with slurred speech and breath that reeked of alcohol, he said, "My name is Tom. What's yours?"

"I'm Mother Hunter, the founder of Love and Charity," I replied.

With that he didn't seem to be surprised or anything, but I could tell that something was wrong, he was preoccupied, something troubling was on his mind. Then he said, "I don't have anywhere else to go, and I don't know what to do. I've never been to a mission before in my life, I feel so ashamed. Can you help me, Mrs. Hunter?" he asked.

"Don't you have family here in Racine, Tom?" I asked.

"Yes, my ex-wife lives here and I also have a son and a daughter that lives here too, but I can't stay with them," he replied. Then he sobbed, saying, "They won't have anything to do with me anymore. They're all I got left in this world, and I can't turn to them, because my drinking has ruined everything between us. I just feel like dying. I'm no good for nothing," he insisted. Then he broke down and cried bitterly. So I began to minister to this heartbroken man, and I said to him "Tom, it's not too late for things to change in your life. If you want help, you can get it right here."

Then he said, "But you don't understand. I can't stop drinking. I've been drinking for over twenty-five years now. I've tried to stop, but I just don't know how. I've been to every alcohol program you can imagine, but nothing seems to work for me. I don't know what do with myself any longer. Just today the police picked me up three times in a twelve-hour period. They took me to a detox center but I've been there so many times they informed the police, there was nothing else that they could do for me, so I had to come here, Mrs. Hunter, because I had nowhere else to go, and had no one to turn to," he tearfully emphasized. Hearing all of this, I felt so sorry for Tom. I've seen so many people, in over their heads drowning in alcoholism. My heart really went to Tom because his addiction clearly tormented him. I told him, "Tom, you've tried everything, and everybody but have you tried Jesus? Let's give the Lord a chance to deliver you from the bottle. He can take away the desire you have to drink." Then I also said, "Not only will Jesus deliver you from the bottle, but he will give you a new heart and a new life, a new walk and a new talk. He'll give you a mind to turn your life around and serve him. Tom if you want your life to change for the better, you can start today right here right now. But you've got to be willing to put that bottle down and turn your life over to Jesus. I know the Lord can deliver you," I insisted.

"Yes! I want to be free," he enthusiastically replied. "Mrs. Hunter, what must I do?" he then asked.

"You must call on the name of the Lord and ask him to forgive you of your sins, and to deliver you from alcoholism. If you ask Jesus to be the Lord of your life, He will save you and then give you the power to stay away from that bottle," I reassured.

"Yes, Mrs. Hunter, I want Jesus to save me and be the Lord of my life," he replied.

"You can accept him right now," I said. "I'm ready, Mrs. Hunter," Tom replied.

So we both got up from the kitchen table and went into the chapel. Then together, we kneeled down on the altar and began to pray, and Tom gave his life to the Lord. As he repented and asked Jesus to deliver him, Tom began to cry like a baby. Tom was crying out to God from the very pit of his heart. They were true tears of repentance. After having alcohol destroy his life for so many years, God delivered this man in minutes. Twenty-five years of torment came to an end that very night.

While Tom thought he was running away from his problems, he ran right into the loving arms of Jesus. Yes, I shared Tom's pain, and he shared my strength, together we shared one another's prayers. When it was all over, Tom had gotten the victory over the devil and was delivered from alcoholism.

As he described his deliverance to me, he said that he felt a warm, wonderful feeling come over his body. As he knelt there on the altar, he could feel the Lord, purging his body. For the first time in twenty-five years, he felt like a new man. He went on to say, "The Lord has lifted a heavy burden off of my shoulders and given me rest. Now I have a reason for living. This was the peace that I had been searching for so long," he said.

The joy that Tom had been looking for in the taverns and bars, he found right here in the chapel of a homeless shelter. Although family and friends alike may have rejected Tom, the love he received here saved his life. It's just like the old Gospel hymn says, "Love lifted me. Love lifted me. When nothing else could help, Love lifted me…"

Ever since the night that Tom was delivered, he became like a self-appointed manager of public relations for the mission. "People need to know what goes on here at the mission," Tom would often say. Just like the grateful leper in St. Luke's Gospel, Tom came back to show his gratitude.

One day Tom told me that he would like to organize an event that would honor me for my work here at the Mission. Tom, along with members of my board of directors, got together and came up with a theme for the event, it was called, "Share Your Prayers." As soon as I heard it, I knew it was from the Lord. Share Your Prayers, is just what the churches and citizens of Racine need to do. We should always be conscious of others when we pray. So often our prayers are only focused on our personal situations, but when we pray for one another, whether it's family, friends, neighbors, or townships, I believe that God moves on everyone's behalf. We should share our prayers, just like the night Tom was delivered from his drinking problem, I shared his burdens through prayer.

Tom and Norman Munson worked closely together in getting the right publicity for the event. They called Pastor Charles Thornhill of the Greater Mount Eagle Baptist Church to be the principal speaker for the gala. During the event an official proclamation by Mayor Stephen Olsen and County Executive Len Ziolkowski, was to be read commemorating November 22 through the 27th as "Louise Hunter-Bowers Week."

As I thought about what all this means, I had to give all the glory to God. Not long ago my family and I were the laughingstock of Racine. People often talked bad about me because I had so many children.

My kids were teased and mocked at school, being told that they were the old nasty Hunters. Over the years, friends disappointed me, but through it all I held on to Jesus and the mission.

There were many days my feelings were hurt standing up for Love and Charity. Those so-called church folks didn't think that I was capable of running a mission. Yet through thick and thin I held on. I fought the good fight of faith and continued to believe God against all the criticism and the odds. Now, look how it has paid off. God is honoring me for being faithful to the work that he called me to do. Just like God told Abraham that for his faithfulness, He would make his name great in the earth. Well, this is what God has done for me. He has made my name great here in Racine County.

As the weekend of the Share Your Prayers event drew closer, on November 15, 1986, the *Journal Times* ran the story about Tom Meanes, and Love and Charity. The article's headline read, Man Helping Mission That Helped Him. The article showed pictures of both Tom and me. The article, written by Karen B. Tancill, told of the official proclamation that was to be enacted during the ceremony, but that wasn't the only thing that caught my attention. What really impressed me was Tom's own testimony. He told how he was delivered from alcoholism right there at the Love and Charity Mission after being unable to find help anywhere else. As I continued reading Tom's story, it emphasized that not only the illiterate and uneducated, end up in shelters and missions, but that hard times and misfortune is an equal opportunity employer. Like Tom's situation, the educated and middle class can also end up with no place to go. Tom's story had a great impact on helping bring the truth about homelessness into the light. To read Tom's own words expressing his gratitude for the help he received from us, was very rewarding and it meant a lot to me.

As the commemoration day drew closer, the entire weekend was full of celebration and gala. On Saturday the 22nd, we held our open house.

Racine's citizens had the opportunity to see what their charitable contributions were being used for. We must have entertained at least two hundred guests that day. It was a real success. However, on Sunday night we had the Share Your Prayers program, which was held at Memorial Hall here in Racine. The hall was packed with over three hundred people that came from all over the state of Wisconsin. They came out to hear the reading of the proclamation, commemorating, November 22 to November 27 as Louise Hunter-Bowers Week. Another highlight of that evening was, the testimonials of the men and women that were helped at the Love and Charity.

Tom Meanes and others gave their testimonials, but there was one that brought the house down that night. It was the testimony of a young lady named Kathy O'Brien, from Aledo Illinois. Before an awestruck crowd, Kathy told about the amazing miracle performed on her eyes after receiving prayers from Louise Hunter, who came to Aledo one summer. While giving her emotional testimony, Kathy told how prayers from Louise helped restore her eyesight. Kathy a mother of five, said that Louise heard about her condition, through an associate that does volunteer work at the mission. Kathy said, that the doctors had classified her as being legally blind, because of two tumors that had grown behind both of her eyes. "When they told me that the condition was inoperable, I didn't know what to do, nor who to turn too," Kathy recounted.

"After hearing about my condition, Louise came to Aledo to pray for me. Before she left, Louise said that the Lord told her to place the hands of one of my children over my eyes for ten minutes while having prayer. So I did this for seven days just as Louise had prescribed, and my eyesight got much better. So when I went back to my doctor for a routine checkup, the doctor was completely astonished at my recovered sight. The condition that my eyes were in, due to the tumors, was supposed to be irreversible. It was truly a miracle that the Lord performed on my eyes through Louise Hunter's ministry."

When Kathy finished her passionate testimony, the entire audience stood upon their feet and began to applaud and cheer. Memorial Hall reverberated with the sounds of excitement and jubilation. In the midst of the standing ovation, Kathy O'Brien broke down in tears and then I ran over to her, and we hugged in a passionate embrace. This was one of the greatest moments of my life. This was also a powerful demonstration of what wonderful works have taken place there at the mission.

To hear the testimonies of the changed lives and miracles was overwhelming. To see the throngs standing to their feet, and to hear such acclamation from the audience was quite exhilarating. As I stood on the stage, flanked by political figures, my family and friends, I felt like the greatest woman in the world. The excitement and adulation of this great event sent waves of joy surging throughout my body. It felt so good to recognized and honored. After all these years of rejection and struggle, now I've been exalted for all to see. Just as the Scriptures say in First Peter, "Humble yourselves therefore under the mighty hand of God, that He may exalt you in due season."[32]

After everyone had given their testimonies, Alderman Owen Davies, representing the Mayor's office read the proclamation, for the Louise Hunter Bowers Week, which was to be celebrated annually from hence forth. The proclamation read:

**Whereas,** Louise Hunter Bowers has attracted well-deserved attention by her humanitarian efforts in the City of Racine, Wisconsin; and

**Whereas,** Louise started a mission in 1970 in her own home, and after successive moves operates it on Douglas Avenue; and

**Whereas,** she provides meals and lodging for the homeless and the poor; and

**Whereas,** over the years hundreds of people, young and old, alcoholics, drug users, and people down on there luck have been fed, clothed, loved and shown there is a better way to live and how to help themselves and

**Whereas**, Louise Hunter Bowers has dedicated her life to serving others and what so many others preach, she practices; and

**Whereas**, while at the mission these people attend prayer service and receive love, counseling and encouragement; and

**Whereas,** Louise Hunter Bowers was presented the prestigious Jefferson Award, by WITI-TV, Milwaukee for her community service;

**Now,** therefore, I, Stephen F. Olsen, Mayor of the City of Racine, in the recognition of Louise Hunter Bowers' great love for the people, especially for those who are down and out, and her strong spiritual commitment to humanity, do hereby proclaim the week of Thanksgiving, November 22-29, 1986 as Louie Hunter-Bowers week in the City of Racine and call public attention to her generous deeds and by this means express thanks to her for her efforts in behalf of the whole community.

To hear this great proclamation detailing my accomplishments at Love and Charity was so surreal. This was truly monumental moment in my life. I have my own holiday. What an honor. I could have never imagined in a million years that this poor country girl from Mississippi could have risen to such status, to have a week dedicated for me. Even though it was not a national or even a state holiday, I'm just as proud that Racine County and the city of Racine took time to recognize the struggle, the work, and my contribution to society.

In the December 4, 1986 edition of the *Shoreline Leader* newspaper, there was full coverage the Share Your Prayers event. To my surprise, a picture of Kathy O'Brien and me embracing, along with another photo with me and other city and county officials on stage together were the featured photos. The headline of the article stated, Hundreds Share Prayers With Louise Bowers. The article focused primarily on Kathy O'Brien's testimony about the miraculous restoration of her eyesight. This was so thrilling because if you tell people about a miracle occurring, they will often shrug it off. However, when the person to whom the miracle was performed tells their own testimony about it that gives the account credibility. Thanks to the *Shoreline Leader*, this miracle and Kathy O'Brien's testimony is a part of history.

Long after the adulation of the Share Your Prayers event was over, Mr. Tom Meanes continued to rally support for the mission. He even put some of his executive skills to work and was instrumental in helping us get Love and Charity's federal tax exemption status. Yes, Tom Meanes certainly wasn't one of those ungrateful ones, but he will always stand out as one of those that returned to say thank you. God bless, Tom Meanes, you will always be one of the special memories of the work that God has allowed me to do here at Love and Charity.

## In Harm's Way

Ever since I began to do a work for the Lord, the devil has always fought against me. He has tried his best to hinder the growth of Love and Charity. This is why I had to stay in constant prayer and learn how to fight the devil effectively. There have been satanic attacks that have been launched at me from every side, but the Lord has delivered me from them all. Because I am doing a work for the Lord, God puts his angels around me to keep me out of danger.

When one considers the crime, drugs, murder and corruption that's so prevalent in today's society, we often ask what can we do to halt these consuming social issues. Although we try to pass laws, increase budgets, elect new state and federal officials, all of these measures are ineffective. Since secular society does not recognize the premises of the Bible, it has no basis to understand what it's really up against. Therefore, it can't effectively fight the real powers behind the evil in our society. The Bible clearly tells us it's not flesh and blood we're fighting against.[33] What this means is that it's not a physical enemy we are opposing. Therefore jails, laws, weapons, and increased budgets are inadequate by themselves.

Although evil is indeed perpetrated by people, the invisible force behind the perpetrators is satanic. As Christians, God has developed a way for us to fight, that's effective against the warring influences of Satan. It's called the whole armor of God. It's the breastplate of righteousness, it's the preparation in the Gospel of peace, it's the shield of faith, it's the helmet of salvation, and sword of the Spirit which is the word of God. With these, a single Christian armed in the power of God and standing on faith, can conquer more than an entire army using today's advanced weaponry.

In the world in which we live, the unsaved can be taken captive by Satan at his will.[34] The devil can manipulate people into doing his evil bidding. Since Satan is powerful as Christians we are warned of persecution from people that are inspired by the devil. In the Gospel of Luke, we find this passage, "And ye shall be hated of all men for my name's sake. But there shall not a hair of your head perish."[35] The reason why I have said all of what I have thus far, is because of one particular incident that stands out in my memory. This incident was like a scene from a horror film however, this was no movie. This was all too real. For right there within the hallowed walls of Love and Charity, I would find myself directly in the path of harm's way.

It all started out on a typical day at the mission. The day-to-day operations were in progress as they normally are. There were many donations to be picked up, there were many people coming in and out who needed food, clothing and other assistance. My volunteer workers were scurrying back and forth from the kitchen to the pantry, and the phone was constantly ringing. The pace was hectic because it was the busiest part of the day.

As I was preparing a food basket for a waiting family, one volunteer interrupted me and said, "Mrs. Hunter, somebody's here to see you."

That's when I looked up and saw this very strange looking young man standing there in our doorway. He was a tall slender white man that appeared to be in his mid-twenties. He had on some old raggedy blue jeans and a dingy white T-shirt that looked as if though he had been wearing it for weeks. He was also wearing one of those hot winter knit caps that was pulled down so far over his head that you could barely see his eyes. I thought, *Who would wear one of those hot knit caps in the middle of the summer?*

He hadn't shaved nor combed his hair recently. His long dirty blonde hair seemed to be gnarled and knotted. He was very unkempt and had a pungent body odor. The minute I saw him I knew something was wrong. I just had one of those gut feelings that there was something that wasn't right about this young man. I had an eerie feeling that this man might even be dangerous.

"What's your name, young man?" I asked. "Jeffery," he replied.

"Well, come on in, Jeffery, and have a seat, I'll be right with you as soon as I finish up this food basket," I said.

So he complied and took a seat. While Jeffery was waiting for me to interview him, he just sat there, watching us as we worked. He was so strange because he had this weird fixed gaze, you could just feel it when he was staring at you. He had a cold and melancholy expression that seemed so lifeless. While sitting there in the kitchen, he never said anything directly to us, but he just kept on muttering something under his breath as if he was talking to an imaginary person.

When you've been in the mission business as long as I have, you get used to seeing some of grotesque conditions that people come to the mission in. Although I have seen worse than him, it wasn't just this man's appearance that troubled me. It was something innate about him that didn't agree with my spirit.

Although he made me very uneasy, I treated him just like any other of our residents. God is not a respecter of persons so neither am I. So I gave him the rules and insisted that he change out of those nasty clothes and take a shower. He didn't really seem to have a problem following those instructions, but when you talked to him, he gave you the impression of someone who wasn't all there.

As the late afternoon was approaching, it was time for our evening prayer services. I sent for all of my men to come down to the chapel as I do every time we have service. At this time, there weren't many men staying at the mission, because it was summer. A lot of men won't come to the mission when it's warm enough to sleep outdoors. Since there were only a few men in the mission at the time, I noticed right away that Jeffery was not in the service. So I asked one of my other men to go upstairs and have him come down right away. After being gone for a minute, he returned and said that Jeffery was on his way down. A few minutes later, Jeffery hastily walked into the chapel and headed straight towards the back row of seats. He slumped down in a chair in the far corner, isolating away from the rest of the men who were seated in the front rows. Jeffery appeared to be very agitated, so he just sat there with his arms folded not moving a muscle. The strangest thing yet was that he was wearing that old ugly black cap, but this time it was pulled down so far that he had to tilt his head back to see. I asked him to remove his hat while he was in the chapel during the worship services. Jeffery grudgingly complied, but continued that strange muttering under his breath.

As hard as I tried, I could never get him to participate in the services in any way. He would just remain in the back row with arms crossed and that old ugly hat pulled down over his eyes. He would never say much but would only mumble some strange kind of jargon all the way through the service. During one service I asked him to come up for prayer, but he refused. Jeffery's strange behavior continued for almost two weeks. It was as though he hated anybody or anything associated with God.

One night I was having a prayer service, but no one showed up this particular evening. I had sent some other men out on a pickup, so I was there praying and praising God all by myself. Soon after I began praying on the altar, I felt a coldness blow through the chapel, like a cold wind from off the lake. Then suddenly I felt another presence in the chapel with me. So I immediately I looked around, but I saw nothing, so I continued to pray. As this cold eerie presence remained in the chapel, I began to pray more fervently, louder and louder, clapping my hands and praising the Lord, but then all of a sudden it seemed to get harder for me to pray. It was like an evil force was literally hanging over my head trying to hinder my prayers. However, I kept calling on the name of Jesus and pressing through in warfare prayer.

As I continued to cry out to the Lord, suddenly the Spirit of the Lord prompted me to turn around and look. I looked up and there Jeffery was standing over me with a butcher knife! His hand was drawn back over his head in an offensive striking position. As I looked into his cold callus eyes, it was like looking into the eyes of death. His face shown an eerie, evil countenance, it was like looking into the face of a demon. In a split second, waves of fear raced throughout my body, my life flashed before my eyes. I then fell back on the altar, frozen stiff with fear. It was just like in a nightmare; I was too scared to run or scream.

Then suddenly with a vengeance he swung his arm downward to

stab me. Quickly I shielded my face. However, his arm stopped in mid-air as if someone or something had blocked him. As I peeked up at him, I could see the knife there in his trembling hand. His knuckles were white from the tight grip. Beads of sweat, formed on his face. He looked like a crazed maniac. Again, he violently thrust downward with the knife, but once again something caught his arm. He was not able to bring his arm down far enough to stab me. As I lay back helplessly on the altar, I shouted out the name of Jesus. Suddenly this young man who was driven by demonic rage, dropped the knife, and raised his hands to the sides of his head, and began to shout in a loud voice, "No! No! I can't, I can't!" He dropped to his knees right there in front of me and began to cry, in wrenching agony saying, "No, I can't. I can't hurt her. I can't hurt her," he repeated in agony.

After seeing him break down so, I knew he was no longer a threat. The coldness left the room. At that point I was no longer afraid of him. I felt compassion for him. I wanted to help him, so I grabbed him and held him, as he kneeled there before the altar. I held him in my arms as a mother holds and a frightened little child.

As he rested his head upon my shoulder sobbing and trembling, and I began to console him with the Love of Christ. Jeffery now being truly repentant just kept on saying, "Mother Hunter, I didn't want to hurt you, but these voices I hear keep telling me to kill you. Ever since the first day that I came here those evil voices kept tempting me to hurt you. Mrs. Hunter, I just want them to stop, please make them stop talking to me, it's driving me crazy, please help me, Mrs. Hunter, please," Jeffery begged.

So I got up from the altar and went around to the pulpit to get my holy oil. After anointing him, I lay hands on him and began to bind the evil spirits that were oppressing him. Jeffery suddenly fell to the floor, and his whole body began shaking violently. I tried holding him down as best as I could, but his body continued to jerk as if he was having convulsions. As I struggled with him on the floor, Jeffery began foaming and frothing at the mouth. The sight was grotesque. As I continued to pray his convulsions began to dissipate, and slowly, Jeffery started coming around. After a half hour of fervent prayer and supplication, God's anointing, destroyed Satan's yokes of bondage in this man's life.

Being delivered from the shackles of darkness, Jeffery was restored to his right mind once again. Ironically, the same man who was under the control of Satan, had now given his life to Jesus. This was a magnificent display of God's awesome power, and a wonderful example of God's amazing grace. It was truly remarkable and nothing short of miraculous.

Though I haven't seen Jeffery for years now, when he left Love and Charity he was no longer hearing those demonic voices. To this day I believe he is doing well. He got a job and is a member of a local church. I know there are those that don't believe in either angels or demons, but despite those who doubt, they are indeed real. I will never forget that night as long as I live because God dispatched His angel to stay the hand of my assailant. For as it is written in the Scriptures, "The angel of the Lord encampeth round about them that fear him, and delivereth them."[36]

## Social Consciousness: A Plea to the Nation

If one could identify a particular type cast for the homeless in America, what would it be? If one could pour certain social economic factors into a mold then, what shape would homelessness take on? The fact is, to the average American the homeless seem to only come in one size and shape. Too many, only drug addicts, winos, prostitutes and the uneducated become the vagrants who end up on our cities skid rows. Although this is an unfortunate perception, the fact is, that's exactly what many people think when asked, who are the nation's homeless? It is stereotypes like these that hinder our response and resolve to meet the challenges that the homeless in America present. Yet it's a growing problem, which has spread into the non-traditional segments of our society. The fact is, many gainfully employed Americans have found themselves out of work, and in need of help from the relatively few shelters and missions across America.

In the advent of unstable economic times, factories and businesses have closed down by the hundreds. The reasons behind these failing businesses range from relocation overseas, to mismanagement of corporate funds. In any case, whenever a business shuts down, economic devastation and poverty follow in its wake. Then that's when people who never dreamed they would need any kind of assistance, find themselves out of work and in desperate need of help.

So when thinking of that common shape which characterizes the homeless here in America, you can get a better idea of what they're like, when you look across your own backyard. Or maybe the best example yet, is a little closer to home. Just look in the mirror and you see what the homeless look like. Yes, that's right, they look like you and me. An increasing number of Americans, who lived in the suburbs and drove imported cars, have found themselves just one catastrophic illness away from financial ruin. So many people who live from, paycheck-to-paycheck, could not stay afloat in the event of a plant closure, or downsizing. Although we're in the richest nation in the world, people are still falling through the economic cracks in record numbers and no one seems to care.

During most of the 1980s, Americans had to get used to some new political terminology. One term was called Reaganomics, and the other was called Graham-Rudman. Both of these ominous terms spelled out financial disaster, and huge budgetary cuts in many of our nations social programs. When it comes down to it, it seems as if though the taxpayers are the ones who reap the whirlwind of budget cuts and bureaucratic red tape. This burden is disproportional and causes the economically disadvantaged to shoulder much of the weight. For example, during the years of the cold war where rhetoric and military posturing prevailed, an increase in military spending was the order of the day. The problem with that seems to be, when military spending is increased, it usually equates to a decrease in social spending. This inevitably means less federal and state dollars to fund domestic programs for those who need it most. Mix these ingredients with a mandate to balance the budget, and the bureaucrats begin to rob Peter to pay Paul.

When the production of weapons of mass destruction has a greater priority than giving aid to our own citizens, it creates painful and insensitive economic circumstances for millions. Consider the corporate corruption, budget cuts, inflation, plant closures, and bureaucratic waste that drain our economy. That means more Americans will inevitably end up without incomes and homeless.

For the average American, the possibility of being homeless is too bitter a pill to swallow. We seem to think of the homeless as nameless individuals who really don't impact our lives. When we see the homeless on the streets, wearing ragged clothing, often carrying all their worldly possessions in a couple of plastic bags, they are often ignored. Usually they draw some harsh criticism and judgmental opinions, like: you're just lazy, or go out and get a job. It's these types of arrogant criticisms that typify the reaction to homeless people, and is a shameful reality that bothers me a great deal.

It's not morally expedient for our government nor its citizens to treat the poor in such crass and cruel ways. As we see more of our citizens living in shelters that are not from the ranks of the undesirable, we should re-evaluate our attitudes concerning homelessness. Certainly, we should not deny aid to those who have washed up on rocky economic shores.

Since dedicating my life for the cause of the homeless, I have received some honor and recognition. Although I never feel as if I have done enough. In 1989 I received an award from the Equal Rights Council of the State of Wisconsin. This award was presented to me in Appleton, Wisconsin, for my work in the area of human rights. However, there was somewhat of an irony that I had to deal with. Of the thousands of people that are helped at Love and Charity every year, many of them are referred to us by the county and the city.

Although they send a lot of referrals our way, they refuse to support Love and Charity financially. The same local governments that are resourceful enough to finance whatever project they want to, will not give a dime to feed or shelter the homeless. Our elected officials should be ashamed and even embarrassed, that they turn their backs financially, to the very mission that they must depend on. It is simply an outrage particularly when one considers the reason why they won't support Love and Charity.

Citing constitutional tenets of separation of church and state, government officials assert that Love and Charity is a religious organization therefore is ineligible for state or federal aid. They also say that if, Love and Charity didn't conduct worship services, we could get funding from the government. If I stopped calling on the Lord in prayer, then I could call on big brother for help. But let it be known from Racine to Capitol Hill, I will never stop worshiping Jesus, nor will I compromise just to get financial aid from the government.

It's a crying shame that the very country that was founded on biblical principles has closed the door on the very truths that made this a great nation. Although the statement "In God We Trust" is written on all of our currency, it's illegal to support a mission that conducts prayer and worship services. I'm afraid America has turned her back on God. In the Bible, we find a passage of solemn warning, "The wicked shall be turned into hell, and all the nations that forget God. For the needy shall not always be forgotten: The expectation of the poor shall not perish for ever."³⁷

I believe that, the day we stop holding prayer services here at the mission, will be the day the Lord's blessings will stop as well. Look what's happened to the schools since prayer was outlawed in the classroom. A commitment to prayer is an essential part of any ministry and is the channel in which God's blessings flow. In order for me to ensure that prayer services continue, I amended our corporate by-laws. The new amendments state that in the event of my death, Love and Charity must remain a Christian organization. This will leave the door open for prayer and worship services to continue. Therefore, even after I'm gone on to be with the Lord, Love and Charity will continue to be run by prayer and faith.

In 1989 a lot of media focus was placed on the homeless here in America. Both political and private activist sat before Senate sub-committees and staged rallies, to raise the national consciousness concerning homelessness. One of the major issues surrounding their protest was, federal and state funds to aid the needy, were being cut across the board while the number of homeless was still increasing. By the time the small tidbits of financial aid trickled down through bureaucratic channels, available funds were depleted even further. In response to this, Americans from all over the nation converged on Washington D.C., to stage a series of protest rallies. Since homelessness is so widespread, it could no longer be considered a major metropolitan issue. The voice of small town America could be heard in cities like Racine, so contingents were sent to the nation's capitol to participate in the protest. According to an article published October 8, 1989 by the *Journal Times*, approximately sixty Racine citizens took part in the national march on Washington D.C.

Although I wanted to participate in that national march, I was not able to get away from the mission at the time. To show our support, I did the next best thing. I organized our own version of the national march, right here in Racine. I really felt it was the right thing to do because I could identify with the day-to-day struggles of being homeless. On the other hand, I could also relate to the complexities of running a mission on a shoestring budget. In order to send a clear message to our city, state and county officials, I called on the support of local political figures, who also had a burden for the homeless. The county supervisor, city alderman and school board members, as well as hundreds of Racine's citizens, all marched from city hall, back to the mission. When some of the marchers and spectators were asked, "What are the causes of homelessness in America?" their opinions ranged from, domestic violence and unemployment, to poverty and drugs. However, the general consensus was the government is not doing enough to address the issue.

As the courageous marchers defied the chilly breeze that blew off of Lake Michigan that cold Sunday afternoon, there was a strong sense of solidarity. School-aged children proudly marched alongside their parents, carrying protest signs, which read: Make Homes, Not Bombs and We The People Deserve, Safe, Decent Affordable Housing. As we marched through downtown Racine, we sang our theme song, "We support the Homeless" borrowing from the melody of the protest song, "We Shall Overcome." As we all marched and sang along together, our cause could no longer be ignored.

This is probably the closest I've ever come to making a political statement. It was high time for our voices to be heard as we spoke out against the U.S.'s unfair social-economic policies. For example, if we can send large sums of financial aid overseas to feed the hungry then why don't we first feed the hungry Americans who live in our own backyard? It's unbelievable that our government will effortlessly pass legislation to save an endangered species of wildlife, yet stonewall attempts to fund shelters for homeless human beings. It's ironic because poverty-stricken people seem to be the real endangered species.

"We Support the Homeless"
Photo by Chuck D'Acquisto, *Journal Times*, Racine, Wis., 10/8/89

It's hard to imagine, but animals seem to get more consideration than socially disadvantaged people. For example, if a whale beaches itself somewhere it becomes national news, but when an increasing number of people are sleeping in the streets, the media won't report that.

In the book of Matthew, Jesus said, "Behold the fowls of the air: for they sow not, neither do they reap, nor gather into barns; yet your heavenly father feedeth them. Are ye not much better than they?"[38] According to the Lord, people are more important than animals. So where have we gone wrong as a nation? How did our priorities get so mixed up? It's time for renewed social consciousness, if America is to continue to be a leader in humans rights among the nations.

These three wonderful vignettes are certainly not all the amazing stories of benevolence, deliverance, miracles, and victories that we have experienced at Love and Charity. However, they are certainly some of the foremost incidences of God's mercy and my resolve to be an effective servant of God, and my most treasured memories.

# Chapter 9
## The House of Hope

In the late 1960s when God gave me the vision to start Love and Charity, I was so eager to fulfill God's will for my life. Although there were many unanswered questions, I trusted that God would equip me to do the work that He called me to do. Through many years of pain and struggle, I watched God supply every need from the greatest to the least. Yes, God proved himself faithful time and time again. I learned that trials and tribulations are what God uses to make our faith stronger. Just as a person who lifts weights gets stronger and can eventually lift more weight, so do the vicissitudes of life make us spiritually stronger so we can handle greater responsibility.

I also came to realize that the more my faith grew, the more Love and Charity was able to grow. For one's achievements can be no larger than the scope of their faith. Yes, indeed it is true that God will not put more on you than what you are able to bare.[39] Through God's manifold blessings, the time had come for me to go to another level in grace and accept more responsibility from the Lord.

When people see me, they often ask, where I get all the energy to handle all the responsibility that I have? In response, I tell them that I trust God to give me the strength, or else I couldn't handle the load. There were many days that I had to do the pickups, the cooking, and the serving and still find the time to raise nineteen children. In addition to all those responsibilities, I manage mission affairs, attend business meetings and make public appearances. I've often asked the Lord, "How much more of this can I handle?" Frankly I wanted no more responsibility because I felt that Love and Charity was more than enough to deal with. However, I soon found out that God saw it differently.

Since I felt that I was doing enough already, I certainly didn't expect God to increase my load. However, I came to understand that faithful service is often rewarded with an increase of responsibility. So often we may think that we are at our capacity in our ministries, our jobs, our careers etc., yet God continues to increase and elevate us. Why? Because God gives us a measure of faith, which coincides with His plans and purpose for our lives. God knows us much better than we know ourselves. It's like what the Psalmist says, "Know ye that the Lord he is God: it is he that hath made us, and not we ourselves…"[40] God gives each person certain abilities and a measure of faith to correspond with our talents. Therefore, He knows what we can handle, and he's also keenly aware of what's too much for us. Unfortunately, we shortchange ourselves by underestimating God and the abilities he has given us. This can actually undermine our faith and hinders us from being as productive as we could be.

When unforeseen circumstances arise in our lives, we quickly find out where our faith is. This is one reason I believe what the Scriptures say, "…for I have learned, in whatsoever state I am, therewith to be content. I know both how to be abased, and how to abound. I can do all things through Christ which strengthens me."[41] What I've spoken of thus far, I had to experience for myself. Right when I thought I had reached a pinnacle in ministry, I found out that God wanted to take me even higher.

In the early spring of 1990, my breakfast program for school kids was in full swing. One morning while serving breakfast, many children came to eat. Any time you have a bunch of kids in one place things can get pretty hectic. My volunteers as well as myself, did the best we could to get the kids fed and on their way to school. I guess you can imagine what it was like, with all those hyperactive children in one room, but by and by we made it through. The last child left for school around eight o'clock. I remember saying, to my volunteers, "It's gonna be another one of those long days. Y'all better sit down and have some breakfast while you can." So I figured I'd take advantage of the slow pace and took a break myself.

There wasn't any prepared food left, so I had to fry my own bacon and eggs. While I was cooking, I began thinking of all the things I had to do that day. There was a food and clothes give away to set up for, and a board meeting later on that evening. As usual, my schedule was absolutely full. So as I sat down to enjoy my breakfast, the quietness that had settled in the kitchen was suddenly interrupted when the phone began to ring. I picked up the phone and said, "Good morning. Love and Charity, can I help you?"

"Yes, may I speak with Mrs. Louise Hunter please?" they asked. "This is she," I replied.

"Mrs. Hunter, hi, my name is Deana Wolfe, I'm an officer at the First Bank Southeast, here in Racine. I'm calling you in regards to a real estate proposition. I thought maybe you would be interested in one of our properties," she said.

Well, I immediately told her that the mission had all it could handle right now, and certainly we don't have the finances to pay on another mortgage.

"No, Mrs. Hunter, the bank wants to donate a house to the mission. It's absolutely free. You see, we have a foreclosure that we wanted to give to someone who'll put it to good use. We really didn't want to sell it to some investor who would rent it out for profit. What we wanted to do was to give it to a nonprofit organization like yours that would make good use of it." Then she went on to say, "Mrs. Hunter, we all admire you for the great work you've done for so many years here in Racine. We all appreciate your tireless efforts therefore, we felt you would be the one who could best use the house. I'll be honest with you, the house needs a lot of work, and it's currently boarded up, but it's structurally sound and it has a good roof."

"Where is this house located, Mrs. Wolfe?" I asked. "It's at 612 Randolph street," she replied.

"612 Randolph street!" I excitedly repeated.

"Yes, that's right, Mrs. Hunter. Is there a problem with that location?" she asked.

"Oh, no, no, don't mind me," I replied. "It's OK. I was just thinking out loud."

Is there something wrong, Mrs. Hunter?" she asked again. "If that location is a problem, I'm sure we can find another property that would be more suitable."

"No, that's all right. It's just that I used to live just a few houses down from that address. As a matter of fact, it's where I started Love and Charity, over twenty years ago right there at 602 Randolph Street." "Well, what an interesting coincidence, Mrs. Hunter," she said. "That's really something isn't it? I guess you never know where life is going to lead you."

"Yeah, you're right about that," I replied.

As Mrs. Wolfe began to go over some of the details, my thoughts began to drift. I wondered what God was trying to tell me in all of this. Why was he leading me right back from where I started? I couldn't figure it out. Why does He want me back in this neighborhood? As

I pondered upon this, I began to recall the memories both good and bad that took place right here on this same old block.

Yes, it was twenty years ago just a few yards down the street, God provided my family with that miracle house. And it was in that same house where God gave me the vision for Love and Charity. It was also this same block where I raised my children, and where my son Thomas died in that dreadful fire. When we left this neighborhood, it was in the aftermath of a tragedy. I thought we had left this neighborhood behind for good. I had no idea that one day I would be returning. I could have never imagined that the path I was on would lead me right back to Randolph Street.

I must admit at first, I didn't want it. I just couldn't see myself as having the time or resources to handle another property. As far as I was concerned, the mission was more than enough. I was convinced that I had gone as far as the Lord wanted me to go, but, at the same time, I didn't want to miss out on what new thing God was going to do. Therefore, I agreed to see the house even though I was having some reservations about the whole thing. Later on that week, Mrs. Wolfe picked me up, and we drove over to the house.

As we turned on to Randolph Street, it was like going back into time. The same old houses and some of the same old families were still living on the block. As we passed by the vacant lot where our old house used to be, it evoked some strong feelings. When we pulled up in front of the house, Mrs. Wolfe smiled and said, "Here we are Mrs. Hunter." I really appreciated her enthusiasm because up until that point, I still had mixed feelings about the whole thing.

As we got out of the car, I began to look over this boarded-up house. Then Mrs. Wolfe said, "I know it's going to need a lot of work, Mrs. Hunter. But I still believe you're the one who can turn this old house into a viable home once again. Well, what do you think, Mrs. Hunter?" she asked.

Part of me wanted to say no, because this house was going to need a major overhaul, but that's when God began to move on my heart, and I began to consider the needs of God's people. I began to realize that it was God who opened the door to get this house, so who was I to turn it down. To top it off, of all the houses that they could have offered, they chose a house that was on the same block where Love and Charity was born. For these circumstances to unfold the way they did, this could be no mere coincidence. God had to be in the plan.

When I took all of this into consideration, I couldn't turn it down. I had to move self out of the way and be open for whatever God was doing. "We'll take it," I said. "I don't know exactly what I'm going to do with it. But, we'll turn this house into a home that someone would be glad to live in. It's time to make a change in this neighborhood. Maybe that's why the Lord has sent me back here."

After our meeting, I began imagining all the things that could be done with that house once it was renovated. My vision was to use the house for men in transition after they'd been released from state correctional facilities. I called a meeting of our board of directors and shared my proposal for the use of the house with the board members. All the board members were very receptive of my idea and gave me one hundred percent of their support. However, as noble as my plans for this house were, I would find out that my vision was not shared with the people in that community. They would meet my plan to turn the house into a transitional living house for ex-felons with fierce opposition. Though I thought I had a good idea, I found out that the road to disappointment is paved with good intentions.

After speaking to the board members about my renovation plans, we focused our attentions on getting a grant to cover the renovations cost. We also had to file a Conditional Use Request to get the property re-zoned for its new intended use. I was requesting that the property be used as a rooming house that could accommodate up to ten newly released adult offenders. When this request was submitted to city hall that's when the wheels of opposition really began to turn. I quickly found out that not everyone shared my vision and enthusiasm for a transitional living facility for ex-felons.

When word of the conditional use request reached the alderman's desk, it was his job to get feedback from all the nearby property owners. According to the city statutes, those who lived within certain proximity of the proposed halfway house could voice their opinions at a public hearing. To my surprise, there was raging opposition to this proposal. In the mean time, the paper work that I had submitted to city hall was forwarded to the city planning commission. It was the responsibility of the city planning commission, to determine what's in the best interest of community and the city as a whole. From their assessment, they would offer a recommendation to the full Council, whether this proposal was in the city's best interest. Then the full Council would have to make the final decision during a public hearing, at which time, all opposing views would be heard. Although there was quite a political storm brewing, I remained confident that the Lord was going to give us the victory.

On June 27th, 1990, the hearing before the full Council, consisting of fifteen city aldermen, heard the opposing testimony of several residents and property owners from Randolph Street. There was one man who voiced his opposition saying that the neighborhood had too many of the wrong elements already. He cited a recent incident that occurred a few months earlier where a woman was found murdered in an abandoned house in the 700 block of Randolph Street. After he and several others voiced their opposition to re-zoning request, the ward alderman read the letters of those who favored the motion.

After everyone spoke before the committee and the council, the planning committee, made its recommendation to deny the re-zoning request. Their reason was, they didn't feel the halfway house was in the best interest of the city nor that community. Therefore, the full council had to reject our re-zoning request, and my plans for housing ex-felons was publicly torpedoed. My initial reaction to the committees denial, was anger and embarrassment. I wasn't used to being defeated when it came to things pertaining to the mission. However, I could have gone on with my plans, anyway. The current ordinance would have allowed me to house up to eight inmates without city approval. If ten was too many, I would have to lower it, I protested. However, in the end, I couldn't ignore the voice of the community. Their concerns were valid. As one resident eloquently argued, she didn't think it should be changed from a residential area, because that's really what it is. "Our community is not for facilities that reform ex-felons, but it's our neighborhood where our children play and go to school each day. Besides," she added, "Those of you who are the proponents of this re-zoning don't live in this community. You live on the other side of town, and wouldn't allow such a facility in your backyard either."

After hearing the passion in which these people made their defense, I had to concede to their positions. I never knew that there would be so many people that would oppose my idea. As the old saying goes, You can't win them all, and so, I had to swallow the reality of losing.

Since God doesn't make mistakes, it obviously wasn't God's will that the house was to be used to house ex-inmates. Though I had the zeal, it wasn't according to knowledge nor the Lord's leading. By losing in the courtroom before the city council, I was compelled to go before the Throne of Grace, to seek God's will in this matter and that's when everything changed.

As I sought the Lord in prayer, the Spirit brought back to my remembrance, the vision the Lord gave me over twenty years ago. In that vision He showed me the children and the elderly that needed to be comforted. Then I also began to recall, the Widow's Closet ministry that the Lord had given me. I remembered the great need of those aged citizens that families and friends had forgotten. I recalled all the joyous gratification that I got when I visited their homes. Then finally I came to the realization that the vision which the Lord was giving me for this house, was part of the original vision He gave me years ago.

Yes, as the Bible says in Ecclesiastes, To everything there is a season, and a time to every purpose under the heaven…a time to break down, a time to build up.[42] The time to tear down, was when we left this neighborhood over a decade ago. But now, it's the time to build up once again. However, this time God wants me to build another type of house, a house that will glorify the Lord Jesus Christ. This shall be a special place for those aged citizens who have lost hope. Indeed, this house shall be a House of Hope. From that time on, I called our new property the House of Hope, a mission specifically for senior citizens.

At last, my bearings were straight, and I was moving in the right direction. As I have done many times before, I was active in raising funds for the renovation work. This house was in such bad condition, it would take months before it was habitable. Soon the word got around that Love and Charity had acquired a property that was to be renovated for senior citizens. Therefore, monetary and material donations from corporations as well as private citizens came in to help fund and support the project. Though the work was progressing and everything seemed to be falling in place, there was a major concern that still hadn't been settled. And that was, who would be the director of the House of Hope? Even though the House of Hope is not far from the mission, I won't be able to be there all the time to run it personally. Whoever I chose for the job would have to be trustworthy because they would have to live there as well.

During the time we had started the renovation, we had just taken in a man named Larry Scheffer. Larry was a retired Korean War veteran that had no place to go. When he came to the mission, he was in really bad shape. He had recently spent several weeks at the VA Hospital in Milwaukee, but was discharged because he started drinking and drugging again. Due to conditions resulting from his chronic alcoholism and heroin addiction the doctors at the VA only gave him six months to live.

For the first few days, Larry acted like he had a chip on his shoulder. He was really cantankerous and very obstinate when it came to the mission rules. But I didn't let his testy disposition bother me, and I wouldn't let Larry get away with anything. However, since I knew he was in a lot of physical and emotional pain, I had compassion on him. As the days and weeks went by Larry's attitude started to change little by little. He became more helpful around the mission, especially when it came to keeping his eyes on things for me. Larry was like a faithful watchdog who became very protective of the mission and me. If there was any funny business going on, Larry wouldn't hesitate to let me know.

Soon it was evident that I could trust Larry and let him care for the mission in my absence. Since the first day that Love and Charity started, I cared for it as it were one of my own children. And as any mother can tell you, we don't leave our children in the hands of people that we don't trust. Larry Scheffer proved himself to be trustworthy. No matter what, he always had the mission's best interests in mind.

One afternoon after Larry returned from doing some pickups, he asked me if he could help out over at the House of Hope. He said, "Mrs. Hunter, when I heard about what was going on at the House of Hope, I just knew that it was for me." He also said that he knew a lot about household repairs and boasted somewhat of being a jack-of-all-trades. Considering how well he had been working out at the mission, I took him up on his offer.

When Larry first started working, I would drop him off, and he'd work on the house alone. Just as he claimed, Larry turned out to be a good worker who worked well on his own. Most of the time I didn't need to tell him what to do because he already knew what needed to be done. Whenever I wasn't tied up elsewhere, I worked right alongside Larry getting things together. Since Randolph Street wasn't in the best of neighborhoods, I thought it would be a good idea for someone to always be on the premises to protect the property. So after we got the inside of the house in pretty good shape, I let Larry move in.

When I saw how faithful Larry was, I sought the Lord in prayer concerning Larry's role at the mission. I took into consideration that he was already getting along well at the House of Hope. Besides, back at the mission the older men, didn't always get along well with the younger men. I guess it was because of the generation gap between them. After all, Larry was old enough to be most of our residents' grandfather. So after months of hard work and dedication, I appointed Larry as the director of the House of Hope, and eventually he was also elected to our board of directors.

Since Larry took over as the director of the House of Hope, I have never regretted it. I'm also proud to say that the Lord did a mighty work in his life. He certainly was a new man, and a great help to me here at the mission and the House of Hope. Whereas the doctors only gave him six months to live, Larry had surpassed their expectations by years. Whenever you would see Larry, there were no signs that he had been through hell and high water. Larry is the perfect example of why the Lord gave me the name, House of Hope. When Larry came to Love and Charity, he was a dying bitter man who had nothing to look forward too. But here at the mission, he found hope. While he had no direction or purpose in life, he found a reason to live on there at the House of Hope. As Larry unselfishly gave himself to the Lords work, God gave Larry the desire to keep on living.

One night I took Larry with me to a fund raiser dinner where I asked him to give his testimony. When he was called on, Larry stood up like the proud soldier that he once was, and walked confidently up to the podium. Larry gave a testimony that brought tears to the eyes of everyone that came that night. He started out saying, "I thank God that I'm here tonight, because if it were not for Him, I wouldn't be standing here before you. If you would have asked me a couple of years ago, Do I believe in miracles? I'm pretty sure the answer would have been, No, I don't. If you would have asked me, Do I believe in God? I would have told you, I couldn't care less one way or the other. But looking back at all the danger that I have been in, to be standing here before you is proof that miracles really do happen.

"Many years ago I joined the U.S. Army and I decided to make it a career. I was a good soldier, I was never insubordinate and I followed orders to the letter. Since I was a model soldier, I moved up in rank really fast. But, I was still your typical G.I., who lived it up with women and booze. When the Korean Conflict started my company was one of the first detachments to be deployed. Our regiment was transported by a naval battle group that escorted us right to the shores of Inchon Korea. "The Korean Conflict was a very bloody campaign. The Korean Rock Soldiers were particularly brutal, and they were very tenacious combat soldiers. Therefore, the fighting was fierce, and there were heavy casualties on both sides. One cold rainy day, a whole battalion of Rock soldiers blitzed our position, there at Inchon Bay. During this massive land assault, most of our company was wiped out. However, many of the survivors were taken prisoner, and I was one of them.

"For the next three years, I lived in a Korean P.O.W. camp. The conditions were horrible and the prison camp guards had no mercy on us. We were often tortured, by various means. The Koreans seemed to enjoy hanging us by the wrist with barbed wire, which was excruciating. When they really wanted to punish us, they would leave us in an open hole for days on end. These holes would quickly fill up with rain, and you would only be inches away from drowning at any given moment. Many men died right there in those watery hellholes. Besides all the horrendous conditions, there were also vermin that ran rampant throughout the prison camp. I often had to fight off the rats that would attempt to eat the ration of rice that the guards would feed us every few days. Some days I was too weak to scare off the rats before they feasted on my food. When that happened it would be several more days before they would feed me again.

"Therefore, to keep from starving we often had to eat whatever we could find. On more than one occasion I ate insects and dog meat. When your options were death by starvation or eat whatever was available, you chose the later. My will to survive was very strong. I was determined not to let the circumstances beat me. I lived on the hope that all the POWs one day would be freed.

"Physically, we were all in bad shape. I witnessed fellow soldiers die of terrible infections that had these awful festering sores. Disease spread among us rapidly, and there was hardly any medical attention. Besides, most of us would have rather died anyway, then to be operated on by one of their butchering prison camp doctors.

"The only thing we had to look forward to, was the heroin that the prison guards let into the camp. At first that was good because it helped us to cope with the pain, resulting from their tortures. But little did I know at the time, the heroin addiction would be the worst torture of them all. Long after we were released from the POW camp, I was still a prisoner to heroin addiction.

"After the U.S., and the Koreans, worked out a prisoner exchange program, I was finally released, but I was hooked on smack, and remained addicted up until I retired in 1958. For years after I had gotten out of the service, all I did was drink and shoot-up heroin. Continuing in that type of lifestyle, soon I was out of a place to live and I had no family or friends to turn to, so I lived in abandoned cars and slept on park benches. Whenever it got cold outside, I would break into homes, sleeping overnight in people's basements. When the morning came, I'd leave.

"After wondering around like that for years, I came to Milwaukee, where I got enrolled in a program for homeless veterans. However, I was only in that program for a few weeks, because I wouldn't stop using and drinking. To make matters worse, right before I left the VA, the doctors told me that I was dying and that I only had six months to live, so I got fed up with the V.A., and left Milwaukee and came to Racine.

"While in Racine I slept anywhere I could. One night I slept in a car that was parked out in front of somebody's house. They must have seen me get into the car because, they came out of the house shooting. Although I tried to get out of the car as quickly as possible, I wasn't fast enough because I was shot in the arm. It really scared me because I thought I was going to die. Fortunately, the man wasn't a good shot, or I would be dead now.

"After I recovered from the bullet wound, I returned to the vagrant life style. I didn't care about myself or anybody else. So I continued to sleep where ever I could lay my head until I heard about the Love and Charity Mission. I went there in hope of finding a place where I could get my bearings straight and then move on. I knew that I only had a few months to live, so my intentions were to spend the rest of my days living it up. Once Mrs. Hunter laid down the rules, I really didn't think I could stay there. I didn't want to abide by the mission's seven p.m. curfew, and I certainly didn't want to attend her religious services. Although I tried to buck the rules, and do what wanted to, Mrs. Hunter wouldn't have it. She had a way of rebuking you that made you feel like you were only two feet tall. Mrs. Hunter was strict indeed, but that was because she loved us, and that was something I needed so badly. I longed for someone who genuinely cared for me.

"So after a while it all started to sink in. And I started to believe in the God that I never wanted a part of. I figured since I didn't have much time left to live, I might as well use the rest of my time to do something positive. So that's when I asked Mrs. Hunter if I could work on the House of Hope. I felt it was the Lord putting it in my heart to help her out, and ever since then my life has never been the same. I thank God for Mrs. Hunter, because if it were not for her, and the House of Hope, I would have probably died somewhere out on the streets. I am grateful to God that He's not a God of a *second* chance, but the God of *another* chance."

After Larry finished his testimony, he removed his glasses and wiped away the tears from his eyes. This was the first time that I ever saw Larry cry. However, these weren't tears of sadness, but they were tears of joy that welled up from a heart of gratitude. When Larry finished his testimony, there wasn't a dry eye in the house. Larry's testimony did a lot for me that night, and I thank God that he sent him to me.

You know I'm so glad that my first plans for the house did not go through. If they would have, I would have never been blessed by Mr. Larry Scheffer's contribution to the mission. Once upon a time, Larry may not have envisioned himself as being an important part of a ministry. Yet God saw Larry's condition and gave him a hope that transformed his life.

Before Larry came to the mission, he was given only six months to live. However, he served at the mission for approximately five years. It was against hope that Larry believed God and the Lord gave him a new life and a reason to live on. From the solitary confines of a Korean P.O.W. camp, to the pits of disparity throughout the United

States, Larry Scheffer found, life, Love and Jesus Christ, at Love and Charity. I thank God for Mr. Larry Scheffer.

In early 1995, Larry Scheffer went home to be with the Lord. Though he is gone, his memory and contributions will live on. Larry's last years of dedicated service contributed significantly to the formation and the daily functioning of this shelter. Because of his commitment to God and the cause of the disadvantaged, others have found peace and refuge at the House of Hope.

## Chapter 10
### The Image of a Godly Woman

What is your definition of a role model? Would your answer simply be, "A person that one could look up to, someone that is greatly admired by others?" Though these definitions partially capture the essence of role modeling, there's a lot more to being a role model than these two meanings. Now don't get me wrong, one should certainly be able to admire or look up to a role model, but unfortunately, people aren't always what they appear to be. I would say that a role model is not only someone that can portray a role, but someone who practices what they preach and is governed by the same principles that they teach to others. Therefore, the best role model is not simply someone who is looked up to, but is also someone who shares their faith through interpersonal relationships with others, and shows good character by a lifestyle that reflects the image of Christ.

Throughout the Bible there are many examples of godly men and women who were excellent role models. However, I would like to examine the lives of two women I think exemplify the term role model. Their names are Lois and Eunice. In the book of Second Timothy we find this passage: "When I call to remembrance the unfeigned faith that is in thee, which dwelt first in thy grandmother Lois, and thy mother Eunice; and I am persuaded that in thee also."[43] Although this is a small passage of Scripture, it really tells us a lot about these two women. If one carefully reads between the lines of this text, you can see, "the faith" being passed down from one generation to the next. As Paul tells us implicitly, their unfeigned or genuine faith began with Lois, was handed down to Eunice, and then also given to Timothy. In the sixteenth chapter of the book of Acts, we also find another reference to Timothy's family. The passage says, "Then came he to Derbe and Lystra: and, behold, a certain disciple was there, named Timotheus, the son of a certain woman, which was a Jewess, and believed; but his father was a Greek: Which was well reported of by the brethren that were at Lystra and Iconium."[44] From these passages, we see that Eunice was a Jewish believer who had a Greek husband. In the ancient cities of Lystra and Iconium, their family enjoyed a good reputation among the Christian community. It is believed that Lois, Eunice and Timothy were probably converted to the Christian faith during Paul's first missionary journey to Lystra. When Paul returned to Lystra on his second missionary journey, he was very impressed with Timothy's zeal for Christ. Therefore, he asked Timothy to accompany him as he continued on his missionary trek.

When studying about Timothy, it is not necessary for us to assume that Lois and Eunice taught him the Scriptures. This fact is recorded in 2 Timothy 3. Speaking of Timothy, the passage says, "And that from a child thou hast known the holy Scriptures, which are able to make thee wise unto salvation through faith which is in Christ Jesus."[45] Although we actually know little about his grandmother and mother, Lois and Eunice, we do know that they were faithful women who taught Timothy the Scriptures. Being God fearing Jewish women, would imply that they were trained in the traditions of their forefathers. They would have been raised observing all the Jewish holy days and feasts. They would have participated in temple worship, offerings and sacrifices, and all other liturgical aspects of Judaism.

Unlike the Scribes (ancient Jewish scholars and lawyers) and the Pharisees (ancient Jewish religious leaders), who specialized in the outward show of righteousness, these women were dedicated to God, not in mere ceremonial practices. This is the type of genuine faith that Paul alludes to when he wrote the second epistle to Timothy. As Paul states, "...I call to remembrance the unfeigned faith that is in thee, which dwelt first in thy grandmother Lois, and in thy mother Eunice..."[43] Here we can clearly see the parent child relationship was the catalyst from which the genuine faith was handed down from one generation to the next. As it says in the Proverbs: "Train up a child in the way he should go: and when he is old, he will not depart from it."[46] Lois and Eunice not only taught the Scriptures, but they were living examples of their teachings. This is the essence and the dynamic of the Christian role modeling and mentoring.

There is a great truth to be considered when we analyze the old saying, *action speaks louder than words*. When applied to the family system, we see the philosophy behind the saying is very practical. As any parent can tell you, it's a struggle to get children to obey you, but more readily, children tend to copy what they see their parents doing, as opposed to not doing what they're told not to do.

For example, if you tell your children not to smoke, that's fine. However, while telling them not to smoke if they see you smoking, your actions have contradicted what you've said. Since parents are a child's first role models, everything that you do, even more so than what you say, could have a lasting effect on your child's behavior. Since it's natural for children to seek their parents' approval, they naturally emulate their parents' behavior. Therefore, what the parents say and what they do, should be consistent.

Just as faith, morals, and character traits can be passed on, so can negative behaviors, attitudes, and perceptions. All these can become multi-generational legacies that ultimately have adverse effects on a child's perception and relationship with God. Therefore, negative themes and roles can perpetuate dysfunctions that are passed down from one generation to the next, and can also have adverse spiritual consequences.

When thinking in multi-generational terms, we should first consider the basic family unit. As defined, the word family means firstly; parents and their children. Secondly, any group of persons who are closely related by blood or ancestry, compose a family. Thirdly, all those persons descended from a common progenitor. Finally, a family can consist of a group of persons that form a single household under one head.

Since we have already examined the family from the perspective of the first definition, lets expand the family concept beyond biological perimeters. As it pertains to the Christian, the Bible tells us that, Christians are born again. This new birth means that God is our spiritual Father, and we are his spiritual sons and daughters, who all make up the family of God. Another way the Bible depicts the concept of the family of God is by the term, "Body of Christ," which is synonymous for the true or universal church. Now as it pertains to the Body of Christ, Jesus is the head of the body (i.e. body of believers). Though God has indeed made us members of His family, via the new birth, He has simultaneously placed his family under the Lordship of Jesus Christ. Therefore, the fourth definition (a family also constitutes any group of people that form a single household under the same leadership), appropriately applies to the church as well.

The concept of the family can be seen, throughout the Bible. In the Psalms, David says, "Behold, how good and how pleasant it is for brethren to dwell together in unity."[47] In the Gospel of Mark, Jesus tells us, And Jesus answered and said, "Verily I say unto you, There is no man that hath left house, or brethren, or sisters, or father, or mother, or wife, or children, or lands, for my sake, and the Gospel's. But he shall receive a hundredfold now in this time, houses, and brethren, and sisters, and mothers, and children..."⁴⁸ Finally, Paul also refers to the union of the husband and wife first sighted in Genesis, as also mysteriously alluding to the relationship between Christ and the church.⁴⁹

As we continue in our study, we find that Paul teaches family principles as it relates to the church. In first Timothy chapter five, The Bible says, "Rebuke not an elder, but entreat him as a father; and the younger men as brethren; The elder women as mothers; the younger as sisters, with all purity."⁵⁰ Here Paul teaches congregational relationships should be patterned after the family, with the same recognition and respect one would give to their natural family members.

At the beginning of this chapter, I spoke of the importance of the Christian role model. Unfortunately, not all Christians are from believing families that teach Christian principles. So where does the Christian in that situation, find their role models? The church. Ideally, the church family should be the model of Christian ethics for individuals who don't have a Christian support system at home.

In most churches, men are usually the ones in the leadership roles. With this being the case, then to whom do the women who also need godly role models turn? Well, I believe that the answer can be found in Titus chapter two. The passage says, "The aged women likewise, that they be in behavior as becometh holiness, not false accusers, not given to much wine, teachers of good things; That they may teach the young women to be sober, to love their husbands, to love their children, to be discreet, chaste, keepers at home, good, obedient to their own husbands, that the word of God be not blasphemed."⁵¹

According to this passage, the older women of the church have the responsibility to teach the young women godly character and virtue. After all, when it comes to the female experience there are several issues that men cannot relate.

Although a man may be able to empathize with his wife during her trials of her pregnancy, he will never know what it's like to have a baby. In regards to the wide range of issues unique to women, it takes an experienced woman to teach the inexperienced women. Therefore, in the church family, the elder women are to be received as the Mothers of the church. And the mothers of the church should project the image of a godly woman onto the younger women in the congregation.

Just as Lois passed godly character onto her daughter Eunice, there have also been women in my life, that have passed on godliness to me as well. My first female role model was my mother, Carrie Strong. From her I learned my first Scriptures, and learned to sing my first Christian hymns. She taught us how to pray and give reverence to God. From my mother, I learned all the basic tenets of moral character.

From my brief encounter with the nurse in Vicksburg, Mississippi, I learned to be real with God, and to be sorry for sin and repent. From the strange woman that warned me of an impending danger, back in Kinson, North Carolina, I learned that God often sends us warning before trouble happens and that He's faithfully provides a way of escape. From the real estate woman in Kinson who was the good Samaritan and brought us groceries and paid our way back to Vickburg, I learned that God is our provider and he also wants us to have compassion on others in need.

Out of all the women that have been beneficial to me in one way or the other, there's one that stands head and shoulders above all the rest. She was Mother Alexander, the mother of our church. For many years I used to attend the Grace Temple, Church of God in Christ, here in Racine, Wisconsin. Mother Alexander was an older woman, who was brown skinned, tall and slenderly built. She was a very faithful and humble servant. Mother Alexander would be at the church every day conducting the prayer services. Boy, did that woman know how to get a hold of God. It was as if she could pray the fire down from heaven. If there was ever a woman that was given over to the ministry of prayer, it was she. She had a heavy anointing and if you wanted someone who could get a prayer through, Mother Alexander was the one to call.

Mother Alexander was full of the joy of the Lord, and she was also a very compassionate woman, who was dedicated to the Lord, her family and the church. Mother Alexander set the pace for all the women of the congregation. Just like any loving mother, she expected her spiritual daughters to follow her examples. Mother Alexander was from the old school, and she was hard on us when it came to sin. She didn't believe in folks being lukewarm. As far as she was concerned, either you were for Jesus or you were against him. It was either black or white with her. There were no gray areas.

Holiness was the standard she went by, and nothing else. When she rebuked you, it was with the word of God, and boy would it cut to the bone. Although sometimes she would appear to be rather harsh, her rebukes were always done in love. For example, if a young woman came to church with seductive clothes on, Mother Alexander would certainly let her know that the church was not the place to attract that kind of attention. Since she loved us, she would tell us the truth. As the Bible says, "Open rebuke is better than secret love. Faithful are the wounds of a friend; but the kiss of an enemy is deceitful."[52]

Mother Alexander didn't have much formal education, so she didn't use big two-dollar words. However, when it was time for her to speak, she got the message across loud and clear so anyone could understand it. She had so much godly wisdom and was full of that old mother's wit therefore, you couldn't pull the wool over her eyes even if you tried.

Whenever she conducted praise and worship services, you could just feel the presence of God in the sanctuary. She would lift up her hands to the Lord and began calling on His name. Then she would start to clap her hands, and start singing out, "Hallelujah, thank you Jesus!" And a spirit of exhortation would fill the church as we all joined in behind her. Her commitment to prayer was amazing. She was a real prayer warrior, with fervent and focused prayers. An effective focused prayer life is what I really wanted to have, but I struggled so much in this area.

The more I learned from her, the more I began to grow spiritually. I started to realize that a committed prayer life, like Mother Alexander had was special. Not everyone is committed to pray like she was. This woman stayed on her knees. She could pray for hours. I remember after one prayer service I asked her, how do I go about having such a dynamic prayer life? She said that the Lord has to give it to you. She said, "This is not just any old type of prayer. This is a ministry the Lord has to give to you. Not everyone can be dedicated to an intercessory prayer ministry." Since Mother Alexander was so yielded to God, the Lord used her in a mighty way. She had a great effect on many women young and old alike. She really took pride in training up Christian women, especially if you wanted to go all the way for Jesus. She use to always say, "Sell out for Jesus."

Whenever we were depressed, or hurting over a domestic problem at home, she had a way of bringing us back to reality. In a frank but humorous manner she would say, "Y'all don't mind giving yourselves to these no good men out here, and they ain't gonna do nothing for you. So you might as well give yourself to Jesus. He's the only man I know who gave Himself for you."

Yes, Mother Alexander certainly had her way with words and was a woman of great faith. She would always encourage us to ask the Lord for what you need, and then believe that you will receive it. Mother Alexander was a very kind person and a cheerful giver as well. She was one of those saints that cared about the needs of others more than her own personal needs.

When I first started Love and Charity, it was mother Alexander that would encourage me when my husband was acting up. It was Mother Alexander that encouraged me to hold on to Jesus when no one else seemed to care. It was Mother Alexander who labored with me in prayer, for the Love and Charity Club. Yes, it was Mother Alexander who saw something in me to do a special work for the Lord, and encouraged me when no nobody else would. I could call on her at any time of day, to get godly advice when I needed counseling. I really loved Mother Alexander, because she was a real woman of God, and she taught us how to be real for Jesus. In the times that we live in now, where everything seems to be so artificial, it's good to know that there are some real saints around that will take a stand for Jesus.

Mother Alexander was certainly a gift to our congregation. Through her life alone, God has touched many people. I feel honored to have had her as my role model and mentor. Although she has gone on to be with the Lord, Mother Alexander will always live on with me in spirit. I thank God for Mother Alexander, a woman of God and a woman of great faith.

As the Bible says in Proverbs, "Every wise woman buildeth her house: but the foolish plucketh it down with her hands."[53] Just as this Scripture suggests, a foolish woman is her own worst enemy. When a woman is foolish, she brings shame and disgrace to whomever she's affiliated. It seems like everyone bears the shame, her parents, her husband and children, even her church. Unlike men, a woman can never afford to be seen in certain types of light, or else she will bring a reproach. For instance, if a man sleeps around, in this society, it's more readily accepted. Some may say he's just sowing his wild oats, but if a woman does the same thing, she's called a harlot. Although this is an unfair and immoral double standard, the fact is that's the way things are. Therefore, the Christian woman must be chaste, honest, and live a life of holiness unto the Lord.

In the Bible, Paul admonishes the women, in the second chapter of Titus, he gives us a list of things that women should be taught by the Mothers of the church. The passage says, "The aged women likewise, that they be in behavior as becometh holiness, not false accusers, not given to much wine, teachers of good things; That they may teach the young women to be sober, to love their husbands, to love their children, To be discreet, chaste, keepers at home, good, obedient to their own husbands, that the word of God be not blasphemed."[54]

One of the first things that Paul list here is to teach the younger women to be sober. This not only means sobriety in the sense of no drug and alcohol use, but to also to think clearly, use sound judgment in all matters. Many women have gotten themselves in a lot of trouble because they placed themselves in the wrong situation. Be sober-minded, use your head, avoid even the appearance of evil. Next Paul says that the woman should love her husband and her children. Marriage is a great responsibility. You're no longer your own anymore when you marry. You must remember that if you do not support your husband, he'll never be the man he could be.

Another very important aspect is that problems and trials act as the glue that holds a marriage together. Most problems don't come to stay because you go *through* these trials. It's in the going through that gets you to the other side of the situation. This is why relationships that are built on lust, do not hold up under the pressures that a marital relationship inevitably confronts.

Behind most successful men, there were supportive wives. If you tear down your husband's ego, you're destroying your own home. Remember, marriage is for the better or for the worse. Even if you're in the situation where your husband is having some problems with Christian principles, still support him. As the Apostle Peter says, "Likewise, ye wives, be in subjection to your own husbands; that, if any obey not the word, they also may without the word be won by the conversation of the wives; While they behold your chaste conversation coupled with fear. Whose adorning let it not be that outward adorning of plaiting the hair, and of wearing of gold, or of putting on of apparel; But let it be the hidden man of the heart, in that which is not corruptible, even the ornament of a meek and quiet spirit, which is in the sight of God of great price."[55] With faith and a meek and quite spirit, difficult husbands can be won over. Remember what the Proverbs says, "...and the contentions of a wife are a continual dropping. It is better to dwell in the wilderness than with a contentious and an angry woman."[56]

Paul then instructs women to love your children. Nothing can replace the mother's love and influence in a child's life. Don't neglect your children, pay them close attention, spend quality time with them. They need your reassurance to feel secure. Children that feel safe, loved and appreciated will have confidence in themselves. This means you'll also have to chastise them when necessary. Remember the goal is to raise kids so they will be God fearing, become independent and be productive citizens one day.

He also tells us that women need to be discreet. Indiscretion from a woman sends the wrong signals. There is nothing worse than a loud, unruly woman. In first Timothy we find a similar teaching: "In like manner also, that women adorn themselves in modest apparel, with shamefacedness and sobriety; not with broided hair, or gold, or pearls, or costly array; But (which becometh women professing godliness) with good works. Let the woman learn in silence with all subjection."[57] As I tell women all the time, humility and holiness is the way. Women have much authority in their femininity, not in trying to take a man's place.

Women also need to be chaste, which means clean, honest and virtuous. Keep yourselves up. Don't let yourselves go. Push that plate back and fast, you'll benefit from it in the long run. Be honest and trustworthy because dishonesty is a hard stigma to live down. No one wants a lying, deceiving woman around them. No one respects a tramp. Take pride in yourselves and be respectable. Be a keeper at your own home. That means to be diligent at your own house. Again the book of Timothy says, "And withal they learn to be idle, wandering about from house to house; and not only idle, but tattlers also and busybodies, speaking things which they ought not."[58]

Remember, if you are minding your own business you won't have time to mind anyone else's business. Women especially need to learn how to keep their mouth shut. Gossiping is a sin and has caused many problems at home, in the community, and in the church.

When a woman possesses godly character, who can't find a more committed and trustworthy person? Once she truly gives her life to Jesus, she's committed for life. A woman's commitment, whether it be to her husband, her children, church, or career, is her God given strength. When a woman commits herself unto the Lord, Christ will reveal Himself to her in a special way. While men tend to be stiff-necked at times, a women's sensitively and dedication, can be her ornament of grace. For example, after the crucifixion of Christ, the disciples were in hiding, afraid and doubting. However on resurrection morning Jesus first revealed himself to a committed woman named Mary Magdalene.[59]

Remember, while women do have their rightful place in the local church, in Christ there is neither male nor female, because we are all one in Christ.[60]

So what's the image of a godly woman? It's a woman who's life reflects the image of Jesus Christ. As it says in Proverbs 31, "Who can find a virtuous woman? for her price is far above rubies. Many daughters have done virtuously, but thou excellest them all. Favor is deceitful, and beauty is vain: but a woman that feareth the LORD, she shall be praised."[61]

# Epilogue

Forty-eight years have come and gone since Louise opened up the Love and Charity club in July 1970. Down through the years, Louise's poignant labor of love has been an arduous journey. However, the payoff has been thousands of changed lives. Starting the Love and Charity Homeless Shelter was worth the pain and heartache and every tear that was shed. If she could do it all over again, I'm sure that there would be things she would do differently. However, Louise understands what the Bible teaches, that the steps of a good man are ordered by the Lord. Through all of her circumstances, she has learned that love is the greatest gift and has the power to overcome the barriers of adversity and opposition.

On May 18th, 2018, an article in the *Journal Times*, informed the citizens of Racine Wisconsin that the Love and Charity Homeless Shelter would be closing its doors after nearly 50 years of serving those in need. The 84-year-old matriarch and mother of 21 natural children, (17 still living) and scores of grandchildren and great-grandchildren, Louise Hunter, said it was time that she let it all go. Perhaps one of her grandchildren could take up her mantle of servitude.

In recognition of serving the community for nearly a half a century, a proposal was set forth before the Racine city council to name Douglas Avenue, the street where Love and Charity was located for decades, to be renamed Louise Hunter Avenue. Though the director of public works characterized getting this proposal passed through city council, as being "difficult," the effort is underway and has a good chance of passing.

On June 14, 2018, Louise celebrated her 84th birthday. It was a very joyous occasion. Many of her children, grandchildren, great-grandchildren along with other relatives, friends and associates alike, all came to pay tribute to this gracious woman and celebrate the life of this great Christian and humanitarian. There are literally thousands of people that have found refuge from the pitfalls and trials of life by passing through the doors of Love and Charity.

One historic event in the lives of the Hunter family occurred in December 2005, when they were featured in the *Dream Girls* issue of Ebony Magazine. Ebony dedicated four pages to Louise Hunter's powerful story featuring a group shot of 15 of the 21 Hunter siblings standing around their mother. This came about through the tireless efforts of Paul Lamar Hunter the 19th child who is a publicity and marketing whiz. There were rave reviews about the Ebony article which catapulted their story onto the national stage. Additionally, Louise and the Hunter family's story has been covered on several national programs such as Tavis Smiley, Roland Martin, and Tom Joyner shows, and in other national magazines like Upscale, Today's Black Woman, and even the National Examiner, just to name a few.

On the other hand, Paul Lamar Hunter is also a published author with a book titled, *No Love, No Charity, the Success of the 19th Child*. Paul has been touring the country as a motivational speaker, appearing on national radio and television programs as well as, being featured in print and online media too numerous to list here. Paul has written a movie script detailing his life of adversity and triumph. Last but not least, another script has been written covering the inspirational story of Louise Hunter, written by the author of this book. It is our desire that both of these great stories make it to the silver screen.

As I write the last lines of this book, there is somewhat of an irony, because I will conclude this work with the words, the end. But rest assured, as far as Love and Charity is concerned, the work will always live on in the hearts of the those she so lovingly inspired. It is with this understanding that this book should most appropriately conclude with a quote from the sacred Scriptures, "Charity suffereth long, and is kind; charity envieth not; charity vaunteth not itself, is not puffed up, Doth not behave itself unseemly, seeketh not her own, is not easily provoked, thinketh no evil; Rejoiceth not in iniquity, but rejoiceth in the truth; Beareth all things, believeth all things, hopeth all things, endureth all things Charity never faileth: but whether there be prophecies, they shall fail; whether there be tongues, they shall cease; whether there be knowledge, it shall vanish away. "And now abideth faith, hope, charity, these three; but the greatest of these is charity" (1 Cor. 13:4-8, 13, KJV).

# THE END

INDEX

Footnotes

1. Proverbs 22:6

2. Psalms 37:23

3. Rev. 3:20

4. 2 Chron. 7:14

5. Matthew 17:20

6. Ps. 46:1

7. Romans. 8:31

8. Psalms 37:25

9. Romans 12:1

10. 2 Cor. 5:7

11. Proverbs. 11:30

12. Ps. 34:8

13. John 3:16

14. Re. 12:11

15. Matthew 25:37-40

16. Ps. 30:5

17. 2 Sam. 12:23

18. Ps. 41:1-3

19. Mark 3:33-35

20. Mt. 22:39

21. Romans 8:28
22. 2 Cor 10:4
23. Ecclesiastes 11:1
24. Galatians 1:10
25. Isaiah 11:6
26. Philippians 4:6
27. Psalms 121:1-2
28. Mal. 3:16-17
29. Heb. 6:10
30. Mt. 25:21
31. Luke 17:11-19
32. 1 Pe. 5:6
33. Eph. 5:10-12
34. 2Ti. 2:26
35. Luke 21:17-18
36. Ps. 34:7
37. Ps. 9:17
38. Matthew 6:26
39. 1 Cor. 10:13
40. Ps. 100:3
41. Philip 4: 12-13
42. Ec. 3:1

43. 2 Timothy 1:5

44. Acts 16:1-2

45. 2 Timothy 3:15

46. Pr. 22:6

47. Ps. 133:1

48. Mark 10:29-30

49. Eph. 5:30-32

50. 1 Ti. 5: 1-2

51. Ti. 2:3-5

52. Pr. 27: 5-6

53. Pr. 14:1

54. Tit. 2: 3-5

55. 1 Pe. 3:1-4

56. Pr. 21:19

57. 1 Ti. 2:9-11

58. 1 Ti. 5:13

59. John 20:1-2

60. Galatians 3:28

61. Pr. 31:30

# About the Publisher

Let us bring your story to life! Life to Legacy offers the following publishing services: manuscript development, editing, transcription services, ghost writing, cover design, copyright services, ISBN assignment, worldwide distribution, and eBooks.

Throughout the entire production process, you maintain control over your project. Even if you have no manuscript, we can ghost-write your story for you from audio recordings or legible handwritten documents. Whether print-on-demand or trade publishing, we have publishing packages to meet your needs. We make the production and publishing processes easy.

We also specialize in family history books, so you can leave a written legacy for your children, grandchildren, and others. You put your story in our hands, and we'll bring it to literary life!

Please visit our website:
www.Life2Legacy.com

Or call us at:
877-267-7477

You can also email us at:
Life2Legacybooks@att.net

**Featured Books**